Redistribution

REDISTRIBUTION

How Can It Work in South Africa?

edited by
PETER MOLL, NICOLI NATTRASS
& LIEB LOOTS

DAVID PHILIP: Cape Town
in association with the
Economic Policy Research Project, UWC

The Economic Policy Research Project at the University of the Western Cape would like to acknowledge the financial support given by the Friedrich–Ebert–Stiftung. Without this help, neither the workshop 'Budgeting for Redistribution' nor the book which resulted from it, would have been possible.

First published 1991 by David Philip Publishers (Pty) Ltd, 208 Werdmuller Centre, Claremont 7700, South Africa

© David Philip Publishers

ISBN 0-86486-201-6

Printed by Clyson Printers (Pty) Ltd, 11th Avenue, Maitland, Cape

Contents

List of contributors

BRIAN KAHN
Project Researcher, Economic Policy Research Project, University of the Western Cape, and Senior Lecturer, School of Economics, University of Cape Town.

LIEB LOOTS
Professor of Economics, University of the Western Cape, and Director of the Economic Policy Research Project, University of the Western Cape.

PETER MOLL
Visiting Scholar, Department of Economics, Andersen Hall, Northwestern University, Evanston, IL 60208, USA.

TERENCE MOLL
Research Associate, African Studies Centre, University of Cambridge, England.

NICOLI NATTRASS
Researcher, University of Stellenbosch.

ANDRÉ ROUX
Professor of Economics, University of the Western Cape.

SERVAAS VAN DER BERG
Professor of Economics, University of Stellenbosch.

Introduction

PETER G. MOLL

This is emphatically a book about hope for the poor of South Africa. In it a group of academic economists present a number of avenues which they believe will lead to redistribution of income and wealth. They also warn against slick 'polevaults to equality' whose unintended effects would ultimately depress the living standards of the poor and exacerbate the country's gross inequalities.

All the contributors to this volume consider that income redistribution from rich to poor to be morally desirable and, in the South African case, politically necessary in order to achieve a stable and democratic society. But all this is easier said than done. There are countless examples of redistributive efforts all over the developing world which have ultimately impoverished their intended beneficiaries. There are also many examples of successful redistribution. The point is to diagnose the problem accurately, and match to it the appropriate redistributive instruments, taking into account the economic side-effects of so doing.

Accordingly the present contributors met in February 1991 in Cape Town with economists from other parts of the world and with representatives of South Africa's communities to exchange their ideas about what instruments should be used. This book incorporates some of the findings of the workshop, which was held under the auspices of the Economic Policy Research Project, University of the Western Cape.

It should be carefully specified what this book is *not*. It does not represent an attempt to cover every possible redistributive instrument available. The amount of material to cover is so enormous that a shortish book aimed at the general public can at best outline the fundamental principles and illustrate these by reference to particular examples, as has been done here. The book is also not intended to be a blueprint in any specific area. The principles outlined here are consistent with a large number of different government budgets, industrial strategies, and macroeconomic policy choices. Laying down rand amounts for this or the other is a stage that will eventually be reached by decision-makers; the concern in this work is the more general one of achieving consistency among development plans in order to ensure that *in the aggregate*, the economic strategy adopted tends to reduce rather than exacerbate inequality and poverty.

In the first chapter, Terence Moll evaluates a large number of microeconomic strategies for redistribution in developing countries. He discusses the redistribution of physical assets to poor people, by means of land reform and nationalisation. He proceeds to examine the modification of market relations in such a way as to raise the amount or prices of assets sold by poor people. This includes small-scale labour market interventions, blanket interventions such as minimum wages, and the encouragement of large firms to carry out developmental objectives.

In the second chapter, Terence Moll discusses in detail the macroeconomic aspects of redistributive attempts in a wide variety of other countries. One of the most important aspects here is macroeconomic balance. He notes that redistributive regimes are often vigorously expansionary, and that this tactic improves growth performance and the income distribution in the short run – but at the cost of inducing balance of payments crises in the long run.

Lieb Loots, in Chapter 3, studies the ways in which the tax system can redistribute or facilitate redistribution. He first considers by how much the overall tax rate in South Africa should be raised. He examines what would be the likely effects of introducing tax reforms along the lines of what was done in the 1980s in the developed countries and in some less-developed countries. He evaluates the viability of four taxes which would fall most heavily on the wealthy: a wealth tax, a capital transfer tax, a property tax, and a land tax. His recommendations amount to a thoroughgoing restructuring of most of the South African tax system.

In the fourth chapter, Brian Kahn focusses on the financing of budget deficits. He analyses trends in the South African government deficit in recent years and explains in detail how financial policies exert their influence on redistribution through their impact on interest rates, the inflation rate and the exchange rate. He examines both the opportunities and the dangers implicit in deficit financing.

In Chapter 5, Servaas van der Berg argues that government spending tended to increase in other countries following the extension of the franchise. He proceeds to discuss the scope for redirecting expenditures in such a way as to target the poor more accurately. He also investigates how much 'free money' there is, viz how much money can be saved by reducing military expenditures and by eliminating apartheid-related ideological expenditures.

In the sixth chapter, Nicoli Nattrass and André Roux argue that one of the chief avenues of redistribution is radical redistribution within each existing vote of the budget. They proceed to outline, in broad terms, how such a reorganisation of spending could be effected in the health budget. They present the case for Special Employment Programmes aimed at creating income-earning opportunities for poor people.

André Roux, in Chapter 7, examines one of the crucial determinants of the distribution of income – employment. After detailing the appalling employment-creation record in South Africa's formal sector since the seventies, he investigates various explanations, including real wage rigidity, slow economic growth, the efficiency wage hypothesis, and others. He suggests various policy alternatives such as state-supported job search and training services, the deliberate fostering of the informal sector, and centralised collective bargaining.

Finally, Peter Moll draws the threads together in the last chapter. He presents a case for feasible redistribution which takes into account both the urgent demands for redress of the majority of South Africa's people and the economic and financial constraints upon redistributive actions by the state.

1

Microeconomic redistributive strategies in developing countries

TERENCE MOLL

There can be little doubt that steady economic growth should be a policy priority for developing countries. In the long run, only through growth can poverty be decisively eliminated and the quality of life be substantially improved for the bulk of their populations. Economic growth on its own, however, is not sufficient for the alleviation of poverty. While economic growth creates the potential for rising employment levels, real wages and state benefits, it does not guarantee them – not within a generation or so, at any rate.

Further, the gradual alleviation of poverty by means of economic growth alone can be vigorously criticised on the grounds of political unrealism and injustice. In fact, a precondition for a stable and democratic society in many developing countries may be the elimination of the worst inequalities in economic power, for which some redistribution of assets or income or both may be necessary. It is vital, however, that the likely effects of redistributional strategies on economic growth, and vice versa, should be understood – and taken into account – by policymakers in advance. In particular, the experiences of other developing countries can provide valuable parallels by which redistributive strategies proposed for South Africa can be evaluated.

Incomes can be redistributed in many ways, each with a range of effects. As Frank and Webb stress, arguments about the relation between economic growth and redistribution are often broad and unhelpful; it is more valuable, they argue, to search for detailed combinations of policies and target groups that will facilitate both income redistribution and growth (1977, p. 12). Accordingly, we begin by examining the microeconomic effects of individual redistributional strategies in a range of developing countries, considering their macroeconomic consequences and effects when carried out together in the following chapter. The notion of 'redistribution' is interpreted broadly, to cover deliberate attempts at reducing inequality in society and/or improving the absolute position of poor people, as well as economic strategies with such effects as by-products.

Redistributional measures are divided into three categories: the redistribution of physical assets, of market-related earnings, and of state revenues and spending, the last being broken down into consumption and investment components.[1] This typology serves to distinguish between measures which work through different channels, and a number of popular tactics are discussed within each category.[2] The effects of these measures are compared in a later section.

REDISTRIBUTING PHYSICAL ASSETS

One redistributional tactic is to shift non-human wealth (land, factories, machines) directly from rich to poor people, for example to divide large estates among small producers, or to transfer large firms to their workers or to the state (presumed to act on behalf of the people). Such a redistribution changes the right to appropriate income-streams from assets, though it may, of course, involve payments of various kinds (e.g. land being partly expropriated and partly purchased, or being paid for by non-transferable government bonds with low or negative real returns). Attempts along these lines have been made in many developing countries, sometimes with redistributional concerns as paramount, sometimes designed to achieve distributional and other goals.

Land reforms

The first category of asset to be considered is land, the most common approach being to redistribute land from large to small farmers.[3] A number of surveys of research on developing countries suggest that output per hectare is usually higher on small than on large farms, because of the more intensive use of land and labour on smaller holdings (Sheahan, 1987, pp. 137–139; Cornia, 1985; Berry and Cline, 1979). In such cases, output could in principle rise considerably in countries with highly unequal land-holdings if land were to be more equally divided among farmers, suggesting a case for productive land reforms.

Many analyses of land reforms support this hypothesis. Despite a transitional decline in output, new small-scale farmers tend to have an impressive efficiency record. Case-studies in Latin America suggest that output on reformed land – under a range of tenancy conditions – usually did not suffer, and if anything tended to rise, as did total employment (Thiesenhusen, 1989, pp. 485–486). Cline finds the same in a range of developing countries (1977, pp. 280–290).[4] Considering some recent cases of land reform across four continents, Ghose stresses that 'the reforms did not cause any significant disruptions in production' (1983, p. 24). In Zimbabwe, there is evidence that land reform had positive effects on output, productivity growth and land use (Weiner, 1989).

A number of qualifications about land reform are necessary, however. Firstly, it is more effective where the new farmers have some agricultural experience and skills beforehand – which usually means reforms work best when people actually working the land take it over, whether they be tenants or farm labourers. Where these skills are lacking, learning processes are slow and output losses are larger. The second qualification about land reform is that a range of expensive complementary state inputs may be required to make it work, including marketing channels, access to finance, research and agricultural extension support (Prosterman and Riedinger, 1987, ch. 7). Thirdly, land reforms often succeed precisely because they destroy pre-capitalist or feudal social structures which impede economic development, creating a dynamic small-scale agricultural sector instead. Indeed, reforming large estates in East Asia and some Latin American countries appears to have been a precondition for rapid economic development (Dorner and Thiesenhusen, 1990). Where farms are already run on a capitalist basis, however, the gains from reforms might be smaller (Selowsky, 1981, p. 83).[5]

Finally, it is common to find that land reforms do not fulfil their redistributional goals. On the one hand, land reforms usually benefit established or middle-level farmers rather than the very poor, with most landless people, for example, being excluded from benefits (Thiesenhusen, 1989, pp. 486–488; Frank and Webb, 1977, pp. 30–31) – though not always (Ghose, 1983, p. 23). Such 'betting on the strong' may be justified as privileging people likely to be able, eager and motivated, but strains the equity principle inherent in land reforms and probably tends to reflect patterns of local political power and activism. Typically, Weiner observes that in Zimbabwe after 1980 the 'progressive' farmers benefited the most from new production and marketing conditions, leaving out the poorest households and perhaps accentuating rural differentiation (1989, pp. 407–409).

A parallel finding is that land reforms are rarely completed. Thiesenhusen notes that in Latin America about 25 per cent of those legally eligible benefited from reforms (1989, p. 487), and vigorous political opposition tended to bog reforms down sooner or later. Sheahan notes that while many gradualist Latin American land-reform efforts 'made headway for a time, … all fell far short of their objectives' (1987, p. 141). Reforms proceeding by means of legal channels can usually be hampered via legal means, especially where local rural organisations are weak or absent (Dorner, 1972, pp. 29–31). In various South Asian cases, legal delays and strategies of changing land records enabled land ceiling laws to be avoided, such that 'very little land could actually be declared surplus and even less actually distributed to the poor' (Ahluwalia, 1990, p. 116). Likewise, in Zimbabwe the post-Independence land reform surge became bogged down by the mid-1980s, owing in large part to the high costs of land purchase and infrastructure (Palmer, 1990, p. 169). Round the world, some of the most vigorous and extensive reform programmes have been achieved only by force or under threat of large-scale social unrest – imposed by America after military defeat on post-war Korea and Taiwan, for example, carried out after the Bolivian and Cuban revolutions, and implemented by a left-wing military government in Peru after 1968 (Prosterman and Riedinger, 1987, ch. 1).

Redistributing non-land assets

The redistribution of non-agricultural resources – usually mines, large manufacturing firms and the financial sector – is more problematic. The usual tactic here is for the state to nationalise firms in order to achieve three main goals.[6] Firstly, there is the intention to correct for various kinds of market failure (e.g. poor capital markets), linked to which is the desire to weaken the monopoly power of small groups of wealthy producers. Secondly, the state may wish to play a more active developmental and planning role in the economy, which will often focus on the activities of large producers, sometimes with the intention of shifting the economy in a socialist direction. Finally, the state may wish to claim the 'surplus' of large firms – profits, which are often repatriated by multinational corporations (MNCs) – and use it in a redistributive fashion. The effects of such strategies can be evaluated at two levels: firstly, issues related to the nationalisation process, and secondly, the general performance of public enterprises in developing countries. The latter is a huge topic and will only be touched on here.

To begin with, consider the practical difficulties which arise in the nationalisation process. Faced with the threat of expropriation which is not fully carried out immediately a new government comes to power, many firms (large and small) are likely to react by resorting to capital flight or internal disinvestment, while foreign firms are less likely to invest or provide loans; all of this hampers future investment and growth (Ascher, 1984, pp. 107–109, 218). Sheahan (1987, pp. 217–218) discusses this problem for Allende's Chile, where many medium-sized firms – faced with the justified threat of advancing state expropriation – reacted by reducing investment and in some cases even closing down beforehand. Similar instances in Sri Lanka before 1975, Portugal between 1973 and 1975 and Tanzania before 1972 are discussed by Morawetz (1980, pp. 354–355). Along these lines, Cauas and Selowsky (1977, pp. 542–552) note that partial nationalisations of industry may affect the expectations of private sector entrepreneurs so adversely that overall investment and profits decline and government resources available for redistributive purposes are reduced.

Secondly, questions arise about the competence of new managers of the nationalised firms; they often lack the necessary training to run enterprises efficiently (Morawetz, 1980, pp. 353–354). At a broader level, in many developing countries nationalised firms end up draining rather than augmenting state resources – because they are not run to make a profit, because workers achieve high earnings claims, or because prices of their outputs are kept low to keep inflation down and subsidise certain industrial or other inputs. As in Eastern Europe, some nationalised firms enjoy a 'soft budget constraint', by which the state cannot allow them to fail, thus inefficient and incompetent management is not punished. Schafer (1983) further observes that the nationalisation of MNCs raises country exposure to direct international and domestic pressures (economic and political) – for example, commodity price changes, difficulties of access to finance abroad, and labour pressures for high wages.

The Chilean case under the radical Allende regime (1970–73) is intriguing precisely because some of the worst errors associated with nationalisation were avoided. A study of new state industrial enterprises between 1970 and 1973 suggests, for example, that wage rises in such firms were slower and the growth of employment faster than in the rest of the economy (Foxley *et al.*, 1979, pp. 206–212). In addition, there is evidence that many nationalised firms with high degrees of worker participation had impressive productivity records (Espinoza and Zimbalist, 1978, pp. 183–188). However, these firms still lacked a firm budget constraint and their rising share of the state budget meant that their performance was not sustainable in the long run, while the productivity evidence is rather weak. In the case of the nationalisation of Chilean copper in 1970, output remained at surprisingly high levels, but problems of escalating wage demands, deteriorating labour discipline, intra-state struggles over the supervision of the sector, inexperienced personnel and international retaliation were all evident (Moran, 1974, pp. 249–253).

Another radical case which reveals the difficulties of nationalisation is that of post-1959 Cuba. Virtually all large and medium-sized firms were nationalised and drastically restructured within a few months in 1961–62. A shift towards rudimentary central planning took place after 1966; budgetary financing was practised, by which all enterprise profits or losses went into the state budget (Zimbalist, 1989, pp. 68–69), while the distribution of wages within the huge state sector was narrowed sharply. The result was a high degree of social equality, with one of the most drastic shifts of income away from the richest 10 per cent of the population ever recorded in the space of a few years. Likewise, Cuba has achieved an impressive performance in terms of social indicators (Mesa-Lago, 1986, pp. 308–311; Stewart, 1985, pp. 73–74). Partly as consequence of such restructuring, however, Cuba experienced periods of slow or zero growth, as in the second half of the 1960s, though recent work suggests even this period was by no means disastrous (Sheahan, 1987, pp. 244–247). It is clear, however, that the economy suffered from major problems of worker incentives and efficiency, leading to many – only partly successful – reforms designed to counteract them (ibid., pp. 248–252; Zimbalist, 1989). In the long term, it seems unlikely that Cuba's growth-path based on state enterprises is sustainable.

Many difficulties arise in the nationalisation process, and the larger the scale of the nationalisation, the more problems to do with business uncertainty and poor management are likely to arise. Ideally, extensive research should be done in developing countries before nationalisations are carried out. The business performance of firms should be inspected and evidence on management and skills required should be collected, while strategies should be designed about payment, the new legal status of the firm, service contracts with old owners, dealing with contractors, etc. (Green, 1978, pp. 56–67). In individual cases this research may be practical, but the problem with large-scale or hurried nationalisations, of course, is that such care is rarely possible.

More generally, the role of public-sector firms in developing countries is open to question. While difficult to evaluate because of the multiple goals they are supposed to achieve (Mallon, 1981), there is evidence that many waste resources through excessively capital-intensive technology and inefficient management, in large part because of the absence of strong and effective state pressures for firms to avoid waste and cover their costs (Jackson and Palmet, 1988, pp. 209–211). Tanzi (1982) discusses 23 developing countries suffering high and persistent budget deficits between 1974 and 1980; in nine cases he reckons high subsidies for public enterprises were to blame (p. 1077 and Table 8). Sheahan observes further that 'in most Latin American countries ... public firms rarely seem able to generate any surplus to use for any purpose at all' (1983, p. 395). A number of examples of this kind are presented by Ramanadham (1984, pp. 125–129, 135–136).

Nafziger claims that African parastatals tend to be wasteful, characterised by low capacity utilisation, high losses and the erosion of capital resources (1988, p. 78). He notes that they do not reduce local inequalities, tending towards overly capital-intensive production methods, corruption and incompetence (ibid., pp. 88–90; cf. Sandbrook, 1988, pp. 171–175; Biersteker, 1987, pp. 277–283). Killick and Commander stress 'the sheer weight of evidence pointing to low efficiency and returns to investment among public sector enterprises in developing countries' (1988, p. 1467; cf. Jones and Mason, 1982). Millward (1988) provides a more questioning view, concluding that the evidence on technical efficiency in public industrial enterprises in developing countries is inconclusive and varies across countries. He notes, however, that such firms tend to be large and unwieldy, and are subject in many cases to incentive problems (pp. 157–158).

Research by Porteous (1990) suggests that various cases of bank nationalisations – France in 1981, Peru in 1987, India in 1969, Chile in 1971 and Mexico in 1982 – did not achieve their stated objectives of state economic control, reduction in economic concentration, and the desire to cater to the needs of sectors normally excluded from the financial system (pp. 44–48). His general case is weakened because he picks some countries which were in economic crisis anyway (Peru, Chile, Mexico), and fails to consider at least one case where a nationalised financial system was highly successful – South Korea. Nonetheless, it is hard to argue with Porteous's conclusions that in the cases he discusses, alternative means of control over financial systems might well have been preferable (ibid., pp. 69–86). He observes, 'bank nationalisation is complex and costly, both in financial and political terms. There is little evidence that it has achieved its economic goals, for reasons which appear inherent in the nationalisation process in a fragile developing economy at least, such as strong opposition, lack of skilled manpower to manage the banks and international pressures' (p. 59).

On a more positive note, nationalisations appear to have enabled some developing states to carry out large industrial and other projects which would not otherwise have materialised. The problem of a fragmented industrial structure (poor capital markets, long time-horizons for investment, and so on) as justifying nationalisation has been stressed by Fine (1990, p. 135), and cases along these lines have been described by Levy (1988). It is not always clear, however, that nationalisation and state enterprise is the most efficient way of achieving such goals.

In a number of East Asian cases, however, state firms have put up an outstanding performance, led by those in South Korea. The share of nationalised industry in GDP rose from 6,8 per cent in 1963 to 9,6 per cent in 1980; these tended to be activities with high backward-forward linkages in which above-average growth stimulated the rest of the economy (Michell, 1988, pp. 91–92). Jones and Sakong observe that 'the public enterprise sector is relatively efficient by international standards,' noting at most a small efficiency gap with regard to the private sector (1980, p. 164). Likewise, nationalised banks controlled over two-thirds of investment resources in South Korea after 1964, and Sen quotes Datta-Chaudhuri as observing that 'no state, outside the socialist bloc, ever came anywhere near this measure of control over the economy's investable resources' (1981, p. 298). State-owned firms in Taiwan have consistently produced around 13 per cent of GDP, have been responsible for around 30 per cent of gross fixed capital formation, and have been consistently profitable, playing a central role in the development of large-scale capital-intensive sectors like petrochemicals, steel and heavy machinery (Wade, 1990, pp. 175–182). However, while the impressive South Korean and Taiwanese public-enterprise records suggest lessons for nationalised firms in other countries (the importance of management training and incentives, the need for firms to cover costs, export performance as encouraging efficiency), they may be virtually impossible to emulate, for reasons related to national political mobilisation, efficient and independent bureaucracies, early shifts towards corporatist political arrangements, and so on (ibid., pp. 337–342).

A general critique of nationalisations is the possibility that they will end up benefiting the middle classes who are politically powerful and entrenched in market relations, rather than poor people. Nationalisation programmes tend to benefit workers in such firms (actual and future), state officials, and firms and households purchasing their inputs, at the expense of other firms and households, those expropriated, and the state budget (especially if compensation was paid) (Foxley et al., 1979, pp. 202–204; Cauas and Selowsky, 1977, p. 556). The former groups are often relatively prosperous; in many developing countries, workers with formal sector jobs are not amongst the very poor in society, and the latter – rural people, the old and children, informal sector and domestic workers – might be unaffected or even harmed by nationalisation. More generally, it is argued that public enterprises in developing countries have failed to achieve their stated income-redistributional objectives, often benefiting mostly well-off people and in some cases worsening the income distribution (Cook and Kirkpatrick, 1988, pp. 17–18; Jones, 1985).

Distributional issues to do with nationalisation have been covered particularly well in the case of the radical Velasco regime in Peru between 1968 and about 1973. A range of redistributive tactics was implemented, including land reforms of various kinds, the shifting of income and ownership towards workers within industrial, mining and fishing firms, restructuring education and other forms of government spending to benefit the poor, more progressive taxes, and so on (Webb, 1977; Figueroa, 1976; Fitzgerald, 1976, chs. 3 and 6). The effects of the asset-redistributing components of this fairly radical restructuring programme on the income distribution have been described by a sympathetic observer as follows: 'All together they apply to 45% of national income, and transfer between 3% and 4% of it to approximately 18% of the country's labour force. This transfer takes place almost entirely within the wealthiest income quartile' (Figueroa, 1976, p. 171).

In other words, these reforms hardly affected the income shares of the poorest 70 per cent of the population. Even if the estimate of magnitudes transferred should be doubled, as has been claimed (Fitzgerald, 1979, pp. 134–135), they are still low; it has also been argued – albeit based on a less thorough investigation – that the post-1968 reforms had virtually no impact on the income distribution (Weeks, 1983, pp. 77–78). Evidence along similar lines for Allende's Chile (1970–73) is given in Moll (1988, pp. 26–27), where it is suggested that policies of nationalising large capital-intensive firms, for example, privileged only around 20 per cent of the industrial labour force.

Perhaps the chief problem with asset redistribution of any kind is that 'physical' assets are not purely physical; invariably they have a strong human knowledge and organisational component. Sometimes the range of skills necessary to use the assets to their full potential will be held by the people who benefit from redistribution (e.g. tenant farmers whose land is given to them), but often are held largely by people whose assets are being expropriated – which is part of the reason they are in charge anyway. It is difficult to 'redistribute' or acquire such skills quickly, but they are vital in using assets to their maximum efficiency, which is part of the reason why the 'surpluses' from expropriating multinational corporations tend to be small or nonexistent.

MODIFYING MARKET RELATIONS

A second form of redistribution involves the state intervening in market processes of various kinds with the intention of increasing the relative amounts or prices of assets sold by poor people, or reducing the costs of items they buy (Adelman, 1988, p. 500). Tactics here might include supporting (or lowering resistance to) worker demands for higher wages, or prodding MNCs to develop stronger links with local labour-intensive firms. The intention is to use market relations to modify the current and future levels of earnings that poor people get from ownership of various kinds of assets – both non-human and human (skills, education, etc.)

All capitalist states provide a legal and social basis for market relations;

while this is usually stable over time, it can be changed – sometimes sharply. In the redistribution literature, such moves are usually seen as acting against the workings of the market to prevent the worst excesses of unrestrained capitalism, typical examples being minimum wage regulations or high taxes on mining activities. It can be argued, however, that the effects of a range of market-related activities should be dealt with here; for example, attempts to lower barriers to entry to small firms may have positive redistributional effects. Three popular sets of policies will be discussed.

Access to markets

The first important case concerns access to markets and barriers to entry. In many developing countries, changes in market relations intended to improve overall efficiency have served as an instrument of redistribution by weakening constraints adverse to both employment and growth (Selowsky, 1981, pp. 75f). Restrictions on market participation – on industrial entry, the urban informal sector, urban business regulations, labour migration – may be ripe for change, often to the detriment of those currently in markets, or to parastatals. Where certain groups monopolise economic activities so as to secure rents for themselves, freer market relations at the microeconomic level can reduce such rents and create new income sources for poor people who are often those most excluded by, and distant from, market relations (Kannappan, 1985). Likewise, correcting for market weaknesses – for example, the lack of access to credit and training by informal producers and small firms, and their lack of social protection – can have equalising effects (Bromley, 1985; Herschbach, 1989).

While not often regarded as an instrument of redistribution, it appears that in many developing countries such competition-encouraging tactics have served to redistribute income and improve efficiency. A typical example is the rapid growth of the informal sector in many countries, often once barriers preventing its growth have been lifted or access to finance has been encouraged (Tokman, 1983). The scope for informal sector growth and redistribution is especially high when the formal–informal earnings differential is large (International Labour Organisation, 1985, pp. 13–18, 41-45). Such growth cannot do much for the overall distribution of income as most rich people will retain their powerful economic positions, but can shift some income towards the poorest of people and create economic opportunities which were lacking before (see country studies in Van Ginneken, ed., 1988; Rodgers, ed., 1989).

The labour market

The second general area for consideration is the labour market. In many developing countries, labour-market measures designed to shift the balance of power between capital and labour towards the latter have been implemented. Typical tools here are regulations governing minimum wages and working conditions, restrictions on firing workers, higher social security payments by employers and policies of allowing trade unions to organise more freely. Moves of this kind are difficult to evaluate, however, depending very much on individual country conditions (cf. Starr, 1982, p. 153).

Some evidence suggests that such labour regulations can work acceptably if done sensitively, flexibly and on a small-enough scale. Minimum wages in sectors where workers have particularly weak bargaining positions, such as monopsonistic agriculture, may help counter the worst labour exploitation if kept at a suitably low level. A number of cases of minimum wages having positive effects on earnings, with small employment costs, are described by Starr (1982, pp. 161–168); most of these did not involve large increases in the total wage bill. A South American example illustrates the parameters at work here. In Peron's Argentina between 1946 and 1948, workers benefited at the ultimate expense of rich farmers, in large part because efforts to raise wages took the form of gradual and selective state intervention in wage negotiations rather than blanket decrees applied without considering profit levels and productivity (Ascher, 1984, pp. 57–58; Wynia, 1978, pp. 44–47). Even so, however, the dramatic rises in real industrial wages – some 42 per cent in 1947–48 (Wynia, 1978, p. 62) – undermined investment and were not sustainable, being partly reversed in 1949–50.

A general case against large-scale labour market interventions is made by Fields (1984), who compares economic development strategies in seven small economies – the four East Asian newly industrialising countries (NICs), Barbados, Jamaica, and Trinidad and Tobago. In East Asia, Fields claims, market-determined wages and costs were kept in line, with beneficial effects – 'All four Asian economies have ... moved out of the stage of labour surplus', enjoying negligible unemployment (p. 78). 'Flexible' (i.e. highly repressive) labour markets lacking worker organisation or restrictions are regarded as central to this process. By contrast, in the Caribbean, state-induced high-wage policies boosted labour earnings in the short run, but ultimately raised input costs and lowered investment, exports and output, thus leading to poor growth performances. High labour costs also slowed employment growth and worsened inequality, creating a gap between fortunate well-paid workers and the unemployed (ibid., p. 81). While Fields fails to consider differing resources available across these societies, let alone historical, social and political differences, it is clear that labour market and export policies in the East Asian NICs have led to an amazing growth in labour demand, reflected in consistently low unemployment rates, rising labour-force participation rates, an improving industrial composition of employment, soaring real wages and sharp falls in absolute poverty (Fields, 1985, pp. 335f). No other developing countries can claim such a record, especially those with extensive wage-raising labour-market measures.

There are a number of problems with large-scale labour-market interventions like those discussed above. Policies are usually aimed at raising the bargaining power and real wage of workers, which will tend to reduce profits and investment by capitalist firms. In the long run, it is clearly desirable that workers should benefit from rising productivity, but it is vital that the balance between wages and productivity be maintained. It might, in fact, be desirable for wages to lag behind productivity for a while, to raise employment, as was done in South Korea (Rao, 1978, p. 386). Secondly, a sharp shift of income towards labour may harm international competitiveness and exports, thereby slowing down the long-run growth of productivity and wages.

Thirdly, controls can clog up the labour market; higher labour costs and greater labour regulation, for example, may encourage firms to shift towards capital-intensive technologies. The crucial factor here is the responsiveness of labour demand to the wage level,[7] about which the literature mostly reflects uncertainty (Cline, 1975, pp. 387–389; Morawetz, 1977, pp. 140–141). While the degree of responsiveness varies between economies and sectors (being higher in labour-intensive agriculture and the informal sector), there is little doubt that in some would-be redistributive cases, employment growth has been reduced. To avoid these effects, minimum wage and other laws should perhaps be complemented by subsidies on the use of labour (Selowsky, 1981, p. 77). Finally, in some cases the macroeconomic expansion which accompanied blanket labour-market provisions led to economic instability and the nullification of the original programmes (discussed in the following chapter). In short, large and effective labour-market interventions run the risk of reducing profits, investment, exports and the efficiency of the labour market, and hence may undermine long-run economic growth. It is not at all clear that 'free' labour markets are ideal in this respect: some corporatist economies like Sweden have used centralised labour–capital negotiations to keep wages and profits in line and unemployment down, with the state helping to guarantee the positions of both parties. Without such a mechanism, however, drastically raising worker power in individual labour markets can lead to disaster.

From a distributional viewpoint, the chief problem with labour-market interventions is that in middle-income developing countries, earnings inequality within the labour force is the most important source of total income inequality, accounting for more than two-thirds of the total, simply because the labour market is by far the largest market in most economies (Fields, 1988, p. 470). Many measures to increase the bargaining power of labour relative to capital raise wages for established workers but weaken the position of less-skilled low-income workers (Starr, 1982, especially pp. 157–158). It is thus vital to take into account all present and potential market participants when evaluating the likely effects of labour-market policies – for example, possible tradeoffs between higher wages and lower employment, with unemployed people often being unskilled, rural, or unable to gain jobs in the informal sector. Griffin and James observe that minimum wage policies in Tanzania reduced inequalities amongst employed people, but widened the earnings gap between the minority of people with formal jobs and the majority of people (especially rural) who were unemployed or self-employed (1981, p. 29). By contrast, it is intriguing to note that a major example of inequality reduction by means of redistribution in Latin America – Cuba – functioned by keeping urban wages constant and raising real rural incomes. This strategy aided equality by benefiting the rural poor and kept urban wage-costs down (Sheahan, 1983, p. 393).

There is evidence from many developing countries that the most effective way of reducing labour-force inequality is to raise the employment levels and earnings of unskilled workers. Such an approach involves three components: reducing labour-market segmentation between the high-wage formal sector of the economy and low-wage agriculture and the informal sector (Selowsky, 1981, p. 78), rapidly raising the demand for unskilled labour, and rapidly raising the supply of schooling (preventing educated workers from earning large scarcity-rents). The remarkable labour-market records of South Korea and Taiwan were based on strategies of this kind, as was the decline in earnings inequality in most now-developed countries between about 1900 and the late 1970s (Freeman, 1982; Phelps Brown, 1978, pp. 81–86, 99).

Many labour-market interventions, however, have disequalising effects. Consider Zimbabwe during the 1980s. Amongst other things, Mugabe's regime attempted to compress the income distribution by limiting salary rises for workers at the top end of the distribution, implementing legal minimum wages, and enacting regulations barring firms from firing workers without considerable effort; these were seen as 'significant pro-labour measures' (Moyo, 1988, p. 210). The salary-rise regulations were difficult to police and were easily avoided by firms – e.g. through raising fringe benefits or accelerating the promotion of high-income employees. This additional control appears to have been ineffective and wasteful (Stoneman, 1989, pp. 39, 42; Durevell, 1989, pp. 17–18). Minimum wages were set at fairly low levels, but may have harmed employment – especially of unskilled workers – in low-productivity segments of agriculture and industry (Muir *et al.*, 1982). Firms responded to the job security legislation by hiring fewer new or temporary workers (e.g. in agriculture), thus the measure was unpopular for businesses (by limiting their activities and clogging up the labour market), probably pushed them in capital-intensive directions, and did nothing for the unemployed and the least-skilled workers (Durevell, 1989, p. 20). These effects have come to be recognised and many labour-market controls were being withdrawn as of the early 1990s. Such labour-market measures may have harmed worker welfare overall; it has been argued that rising unemployment in Zimbabwe had such a negative impact on the standard of living that most other redistributional policies had only small compensatory effects (ibid., p. 16).

Policies towards large firms

A third area of market intervention concerns the relation between the state and large local firms or multinational corporations (MNCs). As alternative to nationalisation, many developing country states attempt to bargain with or guide such firms in various ways, to achieve developmental or distributional ends. For example, the state may encourage firms to export manufactures or to adopt labour-intensive technologies. State influence may be felt through the state taking part-ownership of such firms, bargaining with MNCs before they enter local economies or threatening to expropriate them, or by tax and other concessions. Aharoni suggests (exaggerating only slightly) 'The arsenal of tools available to governments is large enough to control any firm without acquiring ownership in it' (1977, p. 120).

One review of these issues – focussing on MNCs – concludes that developing country states have considerable scope to bargain with large firms. Using a range of examples, Schatz (1981) shows how such negotiation can take place, concluding, however, that social goals like income equalisation and reduced unemployment are more difficult to bargain for than increases in national income, in government revenue and in local technological development (p. 100). Even regarding appropriate technologies, creating local linkages and the employment of local workers, however, some gains have been made, with examples given by Sheahan (1987, pp. 167–169). Along similar lines, the serious encouragement of small-scale job-creating activities might require constraints on advertising and technology by large monopolies, for example, and additional taxes to raise funds to develop small firms (Allal and Chuta, 1982, p. 63).

Perhaps the classic case of a government negotiating with large firms is that of South Korea. The South Korean economy is dominated by a handful of diversified conglomerates – the *chaebol* – which produce a large share of total output and exports. In 1978 the top five produced almost 20 per cent of manufacturing value added, the top 46 producing 43 per cent, both of these shares rising over time (Michell, 1988, p. 95). Using both positive incentives and vigorous sanctions, the state has pushed the *chaebol* into carrying out its development objectives, the most important being soaring levels of industrial exports – initially with a labour-intensive bias, but becoming more technology- and skill-intensive over time. Incentives included differential interest rates (the state controlled the financial system), price and import controls, and direct state instructions (Jones and Sakong, 1980, pp. 101–126; Amsden, 1990, pp. 21–23; Alam, 1989). By rewarding good performers and punishing poor performers, state and private business work together, 'but there is no question of who calls the tune; it is the government' (Mason *et al.*, 1980, p. 485). Likewise, strict controls over foreign investment prevented MNCs from moving into Korea simply to build up markets there, compelling them instead to form partnerships with local firms (thereby transferring technology and skills) and export much of their output (Koo, 1981; Luedde-Neurath, 1984).

A major constraint on such controls over large firms is the administrative capacity of the state. Many developing country states may be outmanoeuvred by large and foreign firms, lacking the skills to bargain effectively.[8] In such situations, however, while close monitoring may be impossible, careful selection of firms wishing to invest, encouraging local partnerships, the hiring of local employees and high levels of exports could push firms in socially desirable directions.

Modifying market relations: conclusion

A range of other market-related initiatives could be discussed in this context, including the use of taxes and subsidies to change structures of relative prices to the benefit of the poor, price controls, the provision of food stamps, and so on (Ffrench-Davis, 1976; Griffin and James, 1981, ch. 3). Based on the above discussion, two general principles regarding the efficacy of market-oriented methods of improving the earnings position of poor people can be hypothesised. In the first place, market-related reforms are likely to work better the higher the rent component of income of those who will suffer from the reforms (often current market participants) and the lower the administrative costs. Taxes on domestic oil production might be easy to administer, for example, and have minimal market repercussions. By contrast, a minimum wage law for domestic servants or the informal sector would be exceedingly difficult to administer, and if implemented, would reduce employment directly. As Frank and Webb observe, 'Competitive markets, with large numbers of dispersed buyers and sellers, are a powerful defense against attempts to divert or appropriate income flows originating in those markets' (1977, p. 20).

Secondly, policies to raise the returns to assets held by the poor are most effective if carried out in conjunction with efforts to raise the demand for assets held by poor people. In most developing countries, the chief asset owned by the poor is unskilled labour, thus development strategies that increase the absolute and relative demand for unskilled labour are likely to benefit poor people the most. As Adelman notes, such strategies are likely to be based on exporting labour-intensive manufactures and/or raising the productivity of labour in low-productivity agriculture (1988, pp. 501–503). However, demand-expanding policies may well conflict with, or be nullified by, price-raising policies which focus on higher wages. It is thus clear that market-oriented reforms should be carefully scrutinised for their likely effects in both the short and the long run.

STATE REVENUE AND SPENDING

The third redistributional category concerns state revenues and expenditure – changing the balance between the two such that poor people are taxed proportionally less than the rich, if possible, but receive a higher share of government spending, and perhaps raising overall levels of spending (e.g. as a share of GDP). On the tax side, tax systems in developing countries are rarely progressive, owing to tax evasion by the rich and a heavy reliance on indirect taxes (Cline, 1975, p. 391). From a redistributional point of view, it seems the tax system as such is not an effective means of redistribution in developing countries (Bird, 1987). It might be preferable to implement an efficient tax system – described as 'one with a broad base, sufficiently simple rules to permit effective enforcement, and moderate marginal tax rates' (Williamson, 1990, p. 16) – and redistribute the revenues by means of government expenditure (see the chapter by Lieb Loots in this volume).

Government spending on poor people can be viewed as falling into two sub-categories. Consumption spending raises the consumption and welfare of poor people now, but does little for their productivity in the future (e.g. food subsidies).[9] By contrast, investment spending raises the future productivity and earning-power of poor people (e.g. provision of rural infrastructure, education).[10] State spending here can yield high returns, in part because poor people face many market weaknesses in trying to invest in themselves, especially weaknesses in the capital market (e.g. they might be incapable of borrowing in order to finance their education – see Selowsky, 1981, pp. 79–84). Some state spending can have indirect productivity effects – for example, the provision of housing leading to better living conditions and shorter commuting hours, perhaps raising productivity and welfare – which should be taken into account where possible (Dopfer, 1979, pp. 219–238).

Government consumption spending on the poor
The subsidising of consumption by developing country states is usually complementary to other state activities, such as health and education programmes, or takes the form of temporary emergency anti-poverty strategies. Efforts of this kind have helped to relieve the most harmful welfare effects of structural adjustment programmes in a number of developing countries in the 1970s and 1980s (Burki and Ul Haq, 1981). There are some cases, however, in which welfare state tactics involving heavy consumption subsidies have been attempted in developing countries. The benefits and problems here are neatly illustrated by the case of Sri Lanka.

A welfare state system began emerging in Sri Lanka in the early 1940s when the economy was at a fairly low level of development (Sen, 1989, p. 777). Improvements in welfare indicators like life expectancy, infant mortality and literacy were impressive (Stewart, 1985, pp. 77–79), especially in the 1940s and 1950s. Consumption transfers – led by food subsidies – took up a high and increasing share of the government budget in the 1960s and 1970s, however, thereby directly undermining government investment, economic growth and employment growth; food subsidies alone came to some 5 or 6 per cent of GDP during the 1963–69 period (Jayawardena, 1974, p. 279; Rothstein, 1976, p. 595). The subsidies were financed partly through heavy taxes on foreign-owned plantations which were left with little to invest and create jobs (Oshima, 1990, p. 63); ultimately they were nationalised.

This case illustrates the problem with consumption subsidies: unless strictly controlled they may consume an ever-rising share of the state budget and harm long-run investment and growth.[11] Sen suggests that Sri Lanka's income redistributional strategies reduced GDP/capita growth somewhat, though still stresses, 'The overall impression is one of a long haul in matching social welfare achievements of Sri Lanka with income growth' (1981, p.

304). Stewart argues that the state could afford such programmes, and that their decline after a more market-oriented government took power in 1977 was due to a political decision: 'When governments are under pressure because of adverse economic circumstances, social programmes represent an easy target' (1985, p. 80). This view can be challenged (Rajapatirana, 1988, p. 1155); it is claimed, for example, that with better targeting of poor people, 'the social accomplishments could have been achieved at less cost, and growth could have been much better' (Isenman, 1980, p. 247). It further appears that the income distribution gradually worsened after the 1960s, though may have become more even again some time after 1977 (Glewwe, 1988, pp. 236–237), raising questions about the long-term egalitarian achievements of the Sri Lankan welfare system. Likewise, some of the poorest people in the country – labourers on tea estates – were almost entirely excluded from the welfare programmes (Isenman, 1980, pp. 244–245).

More generally, a study of seven developing country cases of food rationing illustrates problems with state attempts to distribute food directly to poor people (Griffin and James, 1981, pp. 31–35). In most cases, income levels were taken into account in distributing food, but in none was poverty the main criterion of eligibility. Urban areas were favoured in all the schemes, and given their relative prosperity, 'it is highly likely that in all seven countries … the food rationing system accentuates inequality' (ibid., p. 32). While this view is exaggerated, problems of urban political bias and difficulties in reaching dispersed rural people reduce the potential impact of this form of redistribution.

Government capital spending on the poor
The state investment case is another story. The aim is to raise the value of assets held by poor people, thereby improving their market positions and sometimes yielding high social returns. There is abundant evidence from the developing world that rising levels of state spending in areas like education, health, nutrition, housing, subsidised credit for poor people, rural infrastructure and spending on children can benefit long-run growth and the welfare of the poor, often at a relatively low cost (Ffrench-Davis, 1976). Selowsky (1981, pp. 89–90) argues that some Latin American countries could eliminate poverty within a short period by spending around 5 per cent more of GDP on the poor (health, education, housing, school feeding programmes), at an estimated cost in terms of physical investment forgone of some 0,5 per cent per annum growth in GDP, and probably less since much of this spending would yield returns over long periods.

Likewise, Ahluwalia and Chenery discuss the likely effects of shifting some 2 per cent of GDP in developing countries from the rich towards investments likely to raise the productive potential of poor people directly – provision of credit and physical inputs, investment in human capital, public investment to raise the productivity of the owned capital of the poor (access roads, irrigation), and so on (1974b, p. 227). They suggest that such efforts, if efficiently carried out, would encourage growth and substantially raise the income share of poor people over time (ibid., p. 232), implying that vigorous reformist efforts can in fact change the long-run asset distribution (particularly of human capital) at fairly low costs.

In a number of developing countries, human capital investment strategies have been at the heart of economic development programmes. Often such strategies have not been implemented for redistributional reasons but simply because the long-run returns from human capital seemed higher than from alternative forms of investment. The most vivid cases here are in East Asia, where rapid expansions in education and health spending served to complement strategies of exporting labour-intensive manufactures (Fields, 1985, pp. 349–350; Stewart, 1985, pp. 75–76). In such respects, countries like South Korea and Taiwan can be viewed as strongly redistributive in the long run. There is some evidence that spending on the human capital of children can yield the highest returns as they are an easily identified group and benefit over long periods. Strategies of achieving equality among children include provision of sports facilities, school feeding, preventive medicine and school inputs (books, transport, etc.) (Ffrench-Davis, 1976, pp. 131–132; Cornia, 1984). The problem is, of course, that human capital investments yield returns only in the long run, requiring far-sighted state policies.

The extent to which state expenditures are investment may also depend on the state economic development strategy. A strategy stressing higher education when jobs for educated workers are scarce might simply be wasteful – or harmful, creating economic expectations which cannot be met. During the 1950s, both South Korea and Sri Lanka invested heavily in education, achieving educational levels far above those of other developing countries. In the 1960s and 1970s, Korea followed an export-oriented strategy characterised by rapid growth in employment at all skills levels, and by the 1970s a skills shortage had emerged (Kuznets, 1988, p. 62; Kim, 1989, pp. 43–44). By contrast, due to slow growth and little labour-absorption in Sri Lanka, widespread educated unemployment prevailed in the 1970s, with many educated young people – yearning for white-collar jobs – living on unemployment relief payments (Isenman, 1980, pp. 249–251; Oshima, 1990, p. 63).[12] Accordingly, it is clear that a human capital redistribution strategy should fit in with a country's growth strategy.

Constraints and implications
There are various constraints on fiscally redistributional efforts. Firstly, the government budget cannot be too unbalanced – that would lead to printing money and inflation, or escalating government interest repayments, neither of which is sustainable. Williamson (1990, p. 10) stresses that one of the major policy lessons from Latin America in the 1980s is that the 'permanent' government budget deficit (the long-term relation between government revenue and spending) should be kept firmly under control (he suggests a maximum of 1–2 per cent of GDP), otherwise the eventual macroeconomic

consequences – inflation, debt and ultimately structural adjustment – bring substantial costs. Likewise, rising taxes can undermine economic activity, profits and investment. A second problem with fiscal redistributions is simply that many states lack the administrative capacity to redistribute through the budget. Often administrative costs and inefficiencies are high; where expensive bureaucratic empires result, countries may be better off doing nothing or trying to redistribute through market processes.

Finally, a problem with optimism about government spending is the common finding that 'fiscal redistribution has almost never been a major progressive force' in developing countries (Bergsman, 1979, p. 103; cf. De Wulf, 1975; McClure, 1975). Theoretically, government spending could be made highly progressive, but the lack of success therein suggests that this strategy has rarely been tried with great vigour, and that the urban middle classes tend to be in a position to appropriate the benefits (e.g. health and educational spending) (Tanzi, 1974). Many allegedly anti-poverty subsidies benefit the rich: 'Africa's subsidies to transport, electricity, water, post office, telephone (disproportionately benefiting urban populations, especially affluent ones), and education ... substantially increase inequality' (Nafziger, 1988, p. 105). Ensuring that poor people benefit from government spending may be ultimately a political problem.

These fiscal constraints suggest two implications for policymakers in developing countries. In the first place, perhaps the priority should be to shift the composition of government spending towards poor people, rather than raising spending levels as a share of GDP. A typical strategy here might be the provision of compulsory primary education, rather than free university for those who qualify and are usually privileged to begin with. Other efforts might include preventive rural health care, target-oriented nutrition programmes and subsidies for basic low-income housing (Selowsky, 1981, pp. 84–89).

Developing countries which have undergone structural adjustment programmes during the 1980s provide intriguing evidence here. In some cases, government spending was restructured and often reduced to fit in with macroeconomic constraints, but the welfare of poor people was maintained through the composition of spending being shifted towards them. One approach is: (i) to allocate spending to areas with a high social rate of return (e.g. education, rural infrastructure, health care), rather than those where rates of return are low (defence, prestige infrastructure), and (ii) within areas like education, to spend where rates of return are highest (e.g. primary education) – in both cases, weighting marginal social rates of return by the share of benefits received by the poor (Cornia and Stewart, 1990, pp. 12–15). In Sri Lanka in 1980, for example, the poorest 20 per cent of the population enjoyed 88,7 per cent of total spending on social services, but a mere 8,4 per cent of transport subsidies (ibid., p. 13). If social rates of return were similar across these areas, a slight redistribution of spending could work wonders for welfare.

Secondly, and at a more practical level, poor people can be targeted to benefit from government spending. There is evidence from some countries that well-targeted social expenditures can raise the living standards and productivity of the poor (Blejer and Chu, 1990). Concentrating on easily defined target groups of poor people – poor regions, children and pregnant women, those who will respond to food-for-work schemes – can be a much cheaper way of alleviating poverty than generalised subsidies (e.g. of transport or food) which have high leakages to non-poor people (Cornia and Stewart, 1990, pp. 15–16). Various labour-intensive employment-creation programmes in Latin America in the 1980s appear to have been reasonably efficient, quick, cheap and selective, provided they involved many projects, were decentralised, and aimed at marginal areas (Tokman, 1988, pp. 121–122). Tokman further observes that these programmes did not necessarily reduce unemployment rates because many allegedly non-economically active people took part in them (mainly women), suggesting that they reached an important component of work-related poverty not covered in the official statistics. A range of research on public employment and 'food-for-work' schemes in Asia reaches similar conclusions (Ravallion, 1990, pp. 245–255).

A rather dramatic case of targeting is Chile after 1973. Social expenditure per capita fell by almost 20 per cent between 1974 and 1982, yet there was an improvement in some social conditions – declining infant mortality and undernutrition, for example – due to carefully targeted programmes aimed at vulnerable groups like children and pregnant women (Foxley and Raczynski, 1984; Hojman, 1989). Similar evidence from Zimbabwe suggests that infant and young child mortality fell during the first half of the 1980s, in part because rises in health spending were directed towards poor people, and were often carefully targeted (Davies and Sanders, 1988).

A MICROECONOMIC COMPARISON OF REDISTRIBUTIVE TOOLS

The redistributive tools described above have a range of effects and constraints, the economics of which will be evaluated according to four criteria.[13] Firstly, what effects do they have on productivity? A closely allied issue concerns the administrative constraints on redistributive strategies: do they rely on new and efficient state administrative initiatives? A third pair of questions concerns the redistributive process. How easily can each redistributive attempt be carried out and sustained – or possibly be reversed under a future government hostile to redistributional objectives? Fourthly, who exactly benefits from each kind of redistributional measure?

Regarding productivity, the record is mixed. Subject to the constraints noted earlier, land reforms, some market-oriented policies (e.g. lower barriers to entry) and some strategies to raise the capital of poor people seem to have positive effects on productivity and growth. In the last case, such investments may have lower returns than in alternative areas, though not always (e.g. where government spending compensates for absent capital markets), and work best if they tie in with the overall development strategy.

A number of reforms appear to be productivity-neutral (e.g. some tax reforms, though broadening and simplifying tax structures may lower administrative costs), while others may have small negative effects, at least in the short run (selective and low minimum-wage policies).

Some redistributive policies, however, appear to have calamitous effects on productivity and growth, most notably large rises in minimum wages, drastic nationalisations of industry or large-scale consumption subsidies, owing to problems of inefficiency, inadequate incentives and the undermining of investment in the long run. These may work largely via macroeconomic channels, through raising inflation and weakening the balance of payments, while heavy consumer subsidies may not harm productivity but may eventually drain the state budget. It should be noted, however, that exceptions to almost any rules about the productivity-effects of redistributive strategies can be found, implying that the conditions under which they are applied are crucial.

Administrative weaknesses may be major constraints on income redistributional programmes, especially when new governments take power but need to use the officials and skills of previous governments to carry out decisions. The implication is that the possibility of reactionary officials, incompetent bureaucrats and state opposition should be built into redistributional plans from the start. Likewise, there are strong pressures for redistributive regimes to raise government employment, but new bureaucrats may be inexperienced, incompetent and liable to rent seeking and corruption. In short, there is often reason to expect a redistributive state to be less efficient than the pre-reform state.

Some redistributional strategies work precisely because their additional administrative components are small; land reforms may need few inputs from the state and rely on existing skills, while many market-oriented policies actually substitute for state intervention. Regarding appropriate policies to raise the capital of the poor, the administrative component is crucial; identifying and implementing opportunities for productive investment may be as much of a constraint as the availability of resources (Ahluwalia and Chenery, 1974b, p. 235). Likewise, new managers of nationalised firms may lack skills and have little time to learn them. Often, however, strategies can be devised to minimise increases in administrative input – for example, through combining state initiatives with the select extension of markets. A classic case here is rural employment creation by means of public works programmes, where the target group – poor people who are able and keen to work – selects itself for the programme. Other strategies would be to increase support for certain non-governmental development agencies, or to use existing state structures (e.g. pensions networks) in new and imaginative ways.

Closely linked to this issue is the third question, about the implementation, sustainability and reversability of redistribution attempts. According to Frank and Webb, 'Weaker governments generally attempt to raise wages; stronger regimes are better able to enforce income and wealth taxes; radical governments redistribute property' (1977, p. 28). It can be argued that the strategies followed by 'weak' governments – large rises in nominal wages and government spending – are most easily reversed, often via market channels (when prices simply rise in parallel with wages), or through inducing macroeconomic disequilibria and eventual stabilisation policies. Such weak strategies are characterised by the attempt to give to the poor without taking from the rich, which is bound to be disastrous.

Initiatives like land reform and changing the composition of government spending can be far more effective in the long run. Where land reform efforts created new and important social strata while weakening old landowners, conservative political shifts did not lead to land reform efforts being thoroughly reversed. In the Chilean case, for example, the land reforms of the 1964–73 period were undermined thereafter, but without a reversion to the pre-reform structure of property rights being possible, owing to the political influence of small farmers (Jarvis, 1989). Likewise, policies of raising the capital of the poor are virtually irreversible, especially for human capital; state welfare spending, however, is an eminently available target for later cuts by right-wing regimes or during periods of economic crisis (Cornia and Stewart, 1990, pp. 18–21).

A major problem here is that of political asymmetry. Often taking from the rich leads to opposition, which is not balanced by political support from giving to poor people. One reason for this is that the rich tend to be organised, vocal and powerful, while poor people are politically weak and marginal. Often, too, the poor or the organised working class expect considerably more (and more quickly) than they are given. Reformist redistributional attempts sometimes slow down or come to a halt over time because governments lose support from the rich and upper-middle classes without gaining it amongst the poor (Ascher, 1984, pp. 212–218). A contrasting pattern has been termed 'political trickle-down' (Frank and Webb, 1977, p. 18), by which people benefiting from new schools, functioning trade unions, new tax systems and land redistribution become conscious of the gains from redistribution and will mobilise to defend them. The probability of such an outcome seems higher if poor people were actively involved politically in the income redistributional process (see Griffin and James, 1981, pp. 60–62; Finsterbusch and Van Wicklin, 1989). In fact, many attempts at economic reform and redistribution appear to be longest-lasting precisely where popular political organisations continually bring the welfare of the poor to the fore.

The final issue covered here concerns the social impact of redistributional attempts – on the distribution of income, and on poverty. This problem can be divided into two parts: the effects of redistribution on the rich, and on the poor. Regarding the rich, few redistributional attempts appear to affect their position much. As Frank and Webb observe, 'there seems no way short of radical property redistribution to achieve a significant reduction in very high incomes' (1977, p. 29; cf. Stewart, 1983).[14] Tactics like raising taxes suffer from important market constraints as redistributional tools – for example, the possibility of rich people or their capital migrating abroad, or of markets and prices adjusting to cancel out the original distributional shift.

However, while the shares of income which can be taken from rich people may be small, often they could eliminate absolute poverty – at least in theory – if efficiently channelled to poor people. In many developing countries, incomes are so unequally distributed that a relatively small income redistribution from top to bottom could make a large difference to absolute poverty. As Webb observes for Peru in 1961, 'a selective transfer of 5% of the national income, taken from the top 1%, and given to the first (poorest) quartile, would reduce absolute incomes at the top by only 16% and would double incomes for a third of the population' (1976, p. 24). While Peru is a particularly stark case, income distributional numbers for many countries suggest magnitudes only slightly lower (calculated from Fields, 1989).

The other side of the question concerns the impact of redistributional attempts on the poor. The problem here is simple: redistributional efforts often shift income from the top end of the income distribution towards the middle, leaving people at the bottom virtually unaffected. According to Frank and Webb, 'The principal thrust of redistribution has been an attack on extreme wealth, with a redistribution in favour of organised and urban labour groups that are usually in the top quartile or third of the income distribution' (1977, p. 13). Some examples of this 'redistribution towards the middle' have been mentioned above; in extreme cases, income may actually be redistributed from the poorer half of the population to the richer half (Jones, 1985, pp. 344–345).

There are various reasons why the poorest people are left out of redistributional attempts. Firstly, many governments prefer to 'bet on the strong', shifting assets (or even educational spending) to people with some skills and income already, who may use such assets more efficiently than the very poor (Thiesenhusen, 1989, pp. 486–488). The growth-costs of redistribution may rise if the poorest people are the major beneficiaries. Secondly, redistribution often reflects a shift in power to middle-class reformist elites who are keen to widen access to economic benefits associated with the state, but fail to extend them to the mass of the population (Frank and Webb, 1977, p. 13; cf. Nafziger, 1988, pp. 130–132). The organised urban working class may be in a position to look after itself, but nothing more; as Sheahan observes, 'Urban labour usually identifies "poverty" with itself. The peasants and landless rural labour are out of sight' (1983, p. 408), and are the most difficult to organise to press for their interests. A third problem is that it is often simpler to redistribute within particular sets of market relations, than to people outside them. It is more straightforward to raise wages of workers in newly nationalised firms than to shift income from such firms to the urban informal sector. Likewise, it is easier to redistribute within cities than from cities to the countryside, where the poorest people in developing countries tend to be.

While the political issues here are tricky, there are three important ways in which the economics of redistribution could be made more effective. In the first place, it is vital that redistributors work out beforehand exactly who the poor people are, and why they are poor. Often they will occupy a range of inaccessible positions – geographically dispersed, in hills or far from roads and towns, without regular jobs and in a range of occupations, illiterate – and be poor for different reasons – lack of formal education and skills, women with young children, old and without a pension, handicapped, etc. (Webb, 1977, ch. 2; Griffin and James, 1981, pp. 25–27). 'Target group' strategies may be needed to ensure all are covered, and may be required to complement each other. The efficiency of targeting, in turn, will depend on how well the chosen redistributional mechanism can discriminate (i.e. how much leakage there is to better-off people), and on how concentrated the target group is.

Secondly, strategies can be devised to ensure that poor people will in fact benefit. Various means tests can be used for direct government spending, or market-oriented methods can select the poorest people (e.g. guaranteed low-wage employment on local public works). On practical grounds, it seems that only targeted government spending programmes can ameliorate the worst of absolute povety – for example, rural housing, education, health, pensions. Even where such programmes are inefficient and of low quality, they can make a substantial difference to the living standards and market position of the poorest people (Frank and Webb, 1977, pp. 34–35).

Finally, as noted earlier, most inequality in any economy can be explained by the distribution of labour earnings. Non-human assets are distributed less equally than labour earnings, but labour earnings tend to have a considerably higher share of national income, suggesting a focus on causes and consequences of inequality within the workforce as well as on the asset distribution. Rarely have redistributional efforts had large long-run effects on the wage distribution, perhaps because the central causal factors at work are the functioning of the labour market, the availability of skills, and the growth in demand for labour. There is some evidence from East Asia that the wage distribution is best equalised by the rapid growth of education and employment, as discussed in the following chapter.

CONCLUSION

The microeconomic relation between the redistribution of income and economic growth is complex. Certain redistributional measures are likely to help firm-level growth and productivity, others will harm growth, but the circumstances in which they are applied are crucial. These include the administrative capacity of the state, the extent of ground-level participation in redistributive activities, the scope for political organisation and resistance by the rich, the distribution of poor people and how well policies are targeted to benefit them, and so on.

One major reason why a redistribution–growth tradeoff might not hold is simply that many redistributional efforts do nothing for either growth or redistribution! Large numbers of 'redistributional' tactics have failed to reach poor people, with the rich, middle classes or organised urban working classes benefiting from the programmes instead. Some of the reasons here are economic (e.g. the diversity and inaccessibility of poor people), but the more important problem is political – poor people lack the organisation and mobilisation to ensure that they benefit from redistributional programmes (Bergsman, 1979, pp. 105–108). On the other hand, a number of highly unequal countries have achieved impressive performances in terms of the alleviation of absolute poverty and extension of education and employment opportunities, implying more promise for future generations.

A final note of warning on these issues is necessary. While generalisations about particular redistributive strategies in developing countries seem possible, the national or local conditions under which the strategies were applied are crucial. If lessons are to be learned for South Africa from experiences in other countries, the initial conditions, exact policies carried out and outcomes should be examined in as disaggregated a fashion as possible. Land reforms have been productive in most countries, for example, but it is possible that the initial conditions in South Africa (lack of skilled black farmers, inadequate state support, diversity of tenurial systems) could prevent such an outcome from materialising. In short, lessons from elsewhere are all very well, but they are no substitute for detailed local empirical research.

2
Macroeconomic redistributive packages in developing countries

TERENCE MOLL

In the previous chapter, microeconomic aspects of the relation between the redistribution of income and economic growth in a range of developing countries were discussed. This approach provides only half of the story, however. Analysing the effects of policies in isolation is intriguing but ultimately inadequate, as it is often argued that the costs and benefits of income redistribution will be experienced at a largely macroeconomic level. In this view, it is most useful to know about the effects of redistributional 'packages' – how policies work when they are carried out together and complement each other. In this respect, South Africans have much to learn from the experiences of other developing countries which have applied various policy packages, as the shift to the post-apartheid economy will fall within this mould.

The chapter begins by considering simulation studies which examine the likely economic effects of hypothetical income equalisations, ignoring the problem of how such equalisations are to be achieved. Next, a number of popular redistributional packages are discussed, and their effects on inflation, the balance of payments and long-run growth are considered. Finally, three socio-economic 'growth-paths' based on different views about the redistribution–growth relation are compared.

Theory and simulation studies
One set of macroeconomic studies examines the effects of income redistribution packages on savings levels and the structure of demand in developing countries. According to one view, high levels of inequality are necessary for economic growth as rich people save vigorously, which serves to fund high levels of investment and rapid economic growth. Where lower-income groups save a lower portion of incremental income than higher-income groups, income redistribution may mean slower long-run growth (Cline, 1972, pp. 9–20). By contrast, it is often claimed that in highly unequal economies, income redistribution packages can render the structure of aggregate demand more compatible with the comparative production advant-

age of the country concerned. Income redistribution to the poor might increase the relative demand for essential goods which are seen as labour-intensive, having low import-propensities and being subject to considerable scale economies in production, thus raising the demand for labour and improving future growth prospects (De Janvry, 1981, pp. 45f; Bequele and Freedman, 1979, pp. 317–320).

Empirical research suggests that neither of these views is tenable. It appears that the poor do not save much less of their income than the rich, so redistribution is unlikely to affect savings rates much. An UNCTAD study on the relationship between income distribution and savings rates in 59 countries, for example, found that savings performance was positively related to the equality of the distribution of personal income (Rothstein, 1976, p. 599). Latin American studies suggest the savings effect of redistribution would be only mildly negative (Cline, 1975, pp. 378–385).

Evidence on demand redistribution from a range of countries indicates that the picture here is complex. Poor groups do not always consume relatively labour-intensive products; they may initially consume more food as their incomes rise, raising agricultural imports sharply; and a fall in the incomes of the rich may lower the demand for labour-intensive services (Colman and Nixson, 1986, pp. 81–87). Some studies find that manufactures – even consumer durables – are consumed on a fairly widespread basis by poorer groups in society, and it is improbable that markets are in fact noticeably constrained by an unequal income distribution (Wells, 1977, especially pp. 273–274; Lustig, 1980, pp. 41–42; Paukert et al., 1981, pp. 103–104).

The empirical literature provides scant support for the belief that the redistribution of demand to poor people and the associated shifts in demand and consumption patterns can be a major stimulus to economic growth. Various authors use a range of models and simulations to argue that no general rules about the effects of income redistribution apply, while positive employment effects are likely to be small, at best (Cline, 1972, ch. 7; Cline, 1975, pp. 375f, 395; Arida, 1986, pp. 195–198; Morawetz, 1977, pp. 129–130). This conclusion is strengthened when second-round effects are allowed for – i.e. the inputs necessary to produce the goods bought by the poor. In one case, the redistributional simulation works perversely; for Colombia in 1968, it is shown that the expenditures of the poor tended to increase factor earnings of the rich more than those of the poor, and vice versa (Ballentine and Soligo, 1978, p. 706). Only in extreme cases of income redistribution are the savings and demand effects likely to be large. A modelling exercise for India suggests that a huge decline in the Gini coefficient from 0,46 to 0,27 would raise employment by 8,5 per cent, raise GDP by 5,3 per cent, and reduce growth rates by around 1 per cent per annum (Mohammad, 1981, pp. 139–143).

It appears, then, that the redistribution of demand from rich to poor cannot be an 'engine of growth' in the way often thought of about manufactured exports, for example. The problem is that most of this research focusses on the comparison of a current economy with a hypothetical simulation in which the distribution of income is rendered more equal. It thus fails to take political conflicts into account, nor does it look at the difficult processes of economic transition towards situations of greater income equality. The problem here is simply that the structure of industry would not adapt easily to a changed demand structure.

In the real world, a rapid income redistribution may lead to sectoral imbalances and induce inflation and balance of payments pressures (Colman and Nixson, 1986, p. 82). Production techniques adapt only slowly to changed cost- and demand-incentives in developing economies, such that a shift towards labour-intensive methods of production might be slow and costly. The crucial variable here is the elasticity of substitution of labour for capital. The higher it is, the more easily labour-intensive production methods can be substituted for capital-intensive ones in response to suitable financial or other incentives. Research in a range of countries yields ambiguous and often contradictory results on this issue (cf. Gaude, 1986; Morawetz, 1977, pp. 139–141); in general it seems the elasticity of substitution in industry falls with the level of development of the economy, and is much higher in the long run (more than five years) than in the short. Thus, even if rich and poor people consume markedly different products, increases in efficiency and employment due to a more appropriate structure of demand and relative prices may only be reaped over long periods, and may depend more on political and macroeconomic factors not encapsulated in the 'substitution elasticity' concept.

Redistributive packages: macroeconomic sustainability and coherence
Few efforts at systematic economic restructuring in a redistributional direction last for very long. Often they are reversed by sudden changes in government, perhaps linked to military coups or foreign intervention or both. In many countries, redistributional attempts were effectively undermined long before formal political reversals – crushed between the hammer of the balance of payments and the anvil of inflation. The problem is that income redistributional efforts often lead to packages of policies being followed which simply do not 'fit together' at a macroeconomic level. The resulting inconsistencies can be partially suppressed in the short run, but emerge in the medium run in the form of macroeconomic imbalances, or as slow long-run economic growth. Often it is the effects of such imbalances – soaring inflation, price controls and lengthy queues in shops, eventually falling real wages – which polarise middle classes against reformers, lead to vigorous political opposition, and create the space for right-wing resurgence or military rule.

Macroeconomic balance
The main proximate reason why redistributional packages fail is their inability to maintain macroeconomic balance. Redistributional phases usually

involve vigorously expansionary macroeconomic policies, designed to stimulate the economy, bring unused resources into use and redirect resources towards poor people. In many Latin American countries, for example, it was argued in the 1960s that the distribution of income in society was a major obstacle to growth, and that a change in the structure of demand and output could dynamise the economy (Lehmann, 1978, p. 109). Macroeconomic imbalances like inflation and balance of payments problems were blamed on political conflicts and various 'structural' factors (e.g. an unequal land distribution, an inflexible production structure, a weak government finance position).[1] While theorised in less detail, similar approaches are common in other developing countries.

The extreme version of this story has been termed 'macroeconomic populism'[2] (Sachs, 1989; Dornbusch and Edwards, 1990), and is neatly described by Diaz-Alejandro (1981). In these cases, governments follow strongly expansionary policies characterised by large rises in government spending not covered by revenues, sharp increases in nominal wages, negative real interest rates, and so on. The 'classic' cases include Argentina 1946–49, Chile 1970–73, Peru 1986–89, Brazil 1986–89, Jamaica 1972–80 and Portugal 1973–76 (Sachs, 1989; Morawetz, 1980, pp. 356–358; Boyd, 1988, pp. 15–31). In the first stage of such programmes, many macroeconomic variables look highly satisfactory. Inflation sometimes falls, real wages rise sharply, the welfare of poor people improves, and exports sometimes rise too. The disconcerting features are falling investment levels, a running down of foreign exchange reserves due to rapidly rising imports, and an appreciation of the real exchange rate (the nominal exchange rate usually being kept high to reduce inflation); these features tend to be overlooked or ignored by exultant policymakers.

At some stage the situation gets out of control as the government deficit soars, inflation accelerates and growth slows. Usually governments resort to direct controls (e.g. over foreign exchange and prices) for a while, which may keep the situation in check until imbalances are simply too large to handle. The programmes are usually terminated by the depletion of foreign exchange reserves, leading to balance of payments crises and abrupt stabilisation episodes involving falls in government spending and the government deficit, a large currency devaluation and drastic cuts in real wages; while welfare indicators usually deteriorate sharply.

A classic expansionary case was Chile under Allende in the early 1970s. The Allende administration which came to power in late 1970 advocated a radical approach to what were termed the 'structural disequilibria' of the Chilean economy – the most important of which were income and asset concentration and continual balance of payments pressures. It held that Chile's economic problems could only be overcome by radical social change aimed at national ownership of the productive structure, redistribution of the means of production and income, and an eventual transition to socialism (Sandri, 1976, pp. 198–199).

The immediate priority of the Popular Unity government was to reactivate the economy, said to be suffering from spare capacity of around 25 per cent in 1970, using expansionary wage, fiscal and monetary policies favouring the poor (De Vylder, 1976, pp. 53–54). Under the impact of higher government spending (the budget deficit rose from 2,7 per cent of GDP in 1970 to 10,7 per cent the following year), real wages soared, real GDP rose by around 9 per cent in 1971, and inflation remained stable at around 35 per cent per annum.[3] Gross investment rates declined, however, owing to business uncertainty, opposition and massive capital flight; private investment fell from 43 per cent of total investment in 1970 to around 15 per cent in 1972, while total real investment fell by 58 per cent over this period. Ascher suggests that public sector investment was 'crowded out' by large wage increases (1984, p. 238). By the end of 1971, inventories and foreign exchange reserves had been run down, capacity had been reached in many sectors, and transport and other infrastructural bottlenecks had begun to appear.

Further rises in wages, credit, government spending and the money supply continued into 1972. The GDP fell slightly, owing in large part to steady collapse in the state sector (De Vylder, 1976, p. 154), but the budget deficit rose further, to 13 per cent of GDP; as inflation soared to over 200 per cent, real wages began falling. Deterioration continued in 1973, with inflation zooming up to 600 per cent and a 5,6 per cent fall in real GDP, while real wages fell to 30 per cent below their levels of three years before. By late 1973, in the midst of massive disequilibria, widespread bottlenecks, state enterprises out of control and queues everywhere, economic collapse and a right-wing takeover were sadly inevitable. Lehmann argues that the future tragedy of the Allende regime was guaranteed by its expansionist approach in its first six months of power, particularly its incomes and financial policy; he reckons that external opposition and economic boycotts had little effect (1978, pp. 116–117). Some recent analyses of the Allende period from the left, however, still fail to give economic factors much weight (see Oppenheim, 1989).

A characteristic feature of reformist and radical regimes in many countries is the desire to lessen the influence of the international economy or to rely on the development of local resources; the combination of expansionary macroeconomics and sluggish export growth often destroys such efforts. The balance of payments is the ultimate constraint on expansionary policies, sometimes precipitating abrupt and brutal adjustments. To give an idea of the forces at work, consider Peru under Alan Garcia in the second half of the 1980s. A populist expansionary policy had been followed since 1985, with some apparent success in the first two years, but showing signs of strain by 1988. Late in that year, the balance of payments constraint began to bite; over the next twelve months, the economy was forced to contract until imports balanced exports, leading to a 20 per cent drop in GDP and a 50 per cent drop in real wages (Williamson, 1990, p. 40; Dornbusch and Edwards, 1990, Figure 5). It is possible that vigorous export strategies could have enabled some such balance of payments traumas to be avoided, but these were rarely seriously tried. Part of the reason for this, of course, is that rising export levels would have implied an exporting strategy, a healthy real exchange rate and certain international constraints on the local economy (e.g. regarding levels of real wages – see below).

Macroeconomic populism is characterised by a number of dubious theoretical features (Sheahan, 1983, p. 412). The most general of these is the denial of tradeoffs – the implicit belief, lacking an empirical basis, that a whole range of desirable welfare objectives can be met at once, by means of huge rises in nominal government spending (Sutton, 1984, pp. 41–42). The escalation in nominal demand rapidly outpaces the productive base of the economy, leading to rising inflation or scarcities or net imports or all of these (Griffith-Jones, 1981, p. 187), with poor people often suffering the most in the process; but such possibilities are not properly considered by redistributors.

Secondly, populist redistributors tend to overlook or be antagonistic towards exports and the balance of payments; policies of internal development are stressed, without realising how crucial the external position is to their success. Thirdly, such policies involve an extension of state control in the economy, without proper consideration of questions of the efficiency of the administration. Fourthly, populist economic programmes often do little for rural poverty, tending to emphasise 'holding down food prices or raising wages for urban workers without realisation or concern for what these policies do to rural incomes and production incentives' (Sheahan, 1983, p. 412).

Finally, where disorders appear, they are initially attacked using direct controls which may contain disorders in the short run but often worsen the economic situation when they are inevitably and progressively tightened and eventually fall apart. Macroeconomic imbalances can be managed by means of suitable direct controls (over prices, foreign exchange and so on) only where their magnitude is kept within a tolerable range; where they soar, direct controls become ineffective and costly. An exception to this story is revolutionary Cuba, where demand was kept under control through strict government rationing of consumer goods, thereby preventing excess imports and not reducing investment resources (ibid., p. 393). This approach, however, was possible only in a fairly rudimentary economy, and entailed long-term motivational and efficiency problems: where consumer goods were rationed, for example, and luxuries were unavailable, there was little incentive for people to raise their incomes. In Zimbabwe under Mugabe, a similar pattern appeared, of economic expansion leading to efforts at stabilisation; there, however, extensive direct controls – over foreign exchange, prices, wages, employment, etc. – were used to control imbalances (Durevell, 1989). While keeping imbalances under limits, such controls appear to have harmed resource allocation, investment and growth in the long run and probably were not maintainable; many have been eased recently.

Macroeconomic chaos is by no means the inevitable result of redistributive policies. In Chile between 1964 and 1970, initially expansionary policies led to some imbalances emerging, but were followed by programmes of macro-economic stabilisation (control of aggregate nominal demand) while some other efforts at redistribution – such as land reform – were continued (Sutton, 1984, pp. 27–29). Along these lines, Dornbusch and Edwards argue that expansionary redistributional policies can perhaps succeed if they are kept under strict control, with an early shift towards growth-oriented policies and an 'extremely orthodox' fiscal policy (1990, p. 274).

Macroeconomic balance is not sufficient for economic growth. It is clear, however, that balance is a precondition for growth; without it, economies become destabilised and disaster results. Sheahan (1987, pp. 315–319) stresses that the various parts of the developing economy should 'add up to a sustainable total system'; where breakdowns occur, the long-term costs to society are high. He even suggests that the major difference between successful and unsuccessful redistributionist regimes is simply that the former had more coherent macroeconomic strategies in the long run (ibid., p. 316).

Redistribution and overall growth strategy
In the longer term, the growth strategy in developing countries is bound to limit redistributional options. The redistribution of large foreign-exchange-earning farms, for example, might prevent rapid industrialisation if the farms stop exporting, as the necessary foreign exchange to buy capital goods will be lacking. Another tool of redistribution is the effort to raise formal sector wages, especially for lower-paid workers. Where developing countries have an international comparative advantage in production using unskilled labour relatively intensively, such strategies might negate these advantages and render the gains from trade far smaller than otherwise. An industrial export strategy based on unskilled labour simply cannot work if the price of unskilled labour, relative to capital and skilled labour, has been raised to an excessive level. In short, the growth strategy should be both feasible and compatible with the redistributional strategy adopted.

It is curious to find that the possible role of exports as a source of growth has been underestimated in most redistributional strategies. A healthy exports position is vital to economic growth in developing countries. Exports – especially manufactured exports – help keep the balance of payments healthy, they fund the importing of high-productivity capital goods which are necessary to rapid growth, they provide some discipline on local producers, and they enable the benefits of comparative advantage to be reaped. The link between exports and redistribution policy is central, in two ways. Firstly, a sustainable exports policy is likely to help a country avoid short-run economic breakdowns and grow faster than otherwise, thus creating room for the alleviation of poverty (as well, perhaps, as the reduction of inequality – for example, through distributing human capital in the form of education and health more widely) (Morawetz, 1980, pp. 358–360). Secondly, there is reason to believe that in some cases, rapidly rising labour-intensive exports can speed up economic growth and actually reduce the levels of inequality in society.

The most spectacular cases of developing countries combining growth and redistribution in the long run are, of course, Taiwan and South Korea. Not only have these countries grown exceptionally rapidly for over thirty years, but they enjoy excellent poverty-alleviation records and have experienced some narrowing of their income distributions.[4] A crucial factor at work here was rapidly rising levels of labour-intensive manufactured exports, which appear to have done wonders for employment growth (at some four to five per cent per annum over many years) and the distribution of income. Indeed, these countries have virtually eliminated poverty, they enjoy unemployment levels of below 3 per cent of the labour force, and have enjoyed amongst the fastest rises in real wages ever known over the past 20 years.[5]

The East Asian NICs are unique in many ways and aspects of their experience cannot be repeated by other developing countries. Their main lesson, however, seems generalisable: that an excessive reliance on import substitution can be wasteful of resources, particularly of labour resources. It is often argued that a greater degree of outward-orientation in closed economies should encourage employment growth by stimulating output growth and a shifting commodity composition of output toward more labour-using activities (cf. Krueger, 1984, pp 146-147, 186; also 1988, pp 368-371). Balassa claims bluntly that export-orientation 'brings larger gains in employment, wages, and income distribution than a strategy of inward orientation' (1988, p 35). While he is a strong optimist, this view should be taken seriously.

One problem with an exporting strategy – especially of manufactured exports – is that pressures are created, pulling domestic prices and wages into line with international prices. In a highly open economy, domestic prices must be aligned with external price structures, disallowing strategies like keeping basic food prices low or maintaining high relative prices for luxury consumer durables. However, countries may be able to combine a vigorous export-orientation with strategies of subsidising basic food prices or combining high internal taxes with high tariffs on luxury goods. Sheahan discusses approaches of this kind in Colombia, Brazil and Mexico, which perhaps limit the growth of industrial exports slightly but leave 'more space for internal choices with respect to structures of production and distribution' (1987, p. 160).

The problem, of course, is that – given reasonably functioning factor markets – most developing countries have a comparative advantage in producing with unskilled labour.[6] Where unskilled wages (or the real exchange rate) are too high, an exporting strategy may be unviable (Krueger, 1988, pp. 373–374). It is thus sometimes argued that an export-oriented strategy implies conservative, repressive politics, to ensure a flexible low-wage labour force and the suppression of worker organisation (cf. Amsden,

1990), thus an export orientation may not be compatible with a democratic, redistributionist society. Many of the most successful developing country exporters – led by South Korea and Taiwan – have been vigorously repressive, with the destruction of labour organisations being particularly high on their agendas. Likewise, Sheahan (1987, ch. 12) coins the term 'market authoritarian' to describe the new export-oriented regimes in the Southern Cone of Latin America which emerged in the 1970s. The general case here, however, is dubious. After surveying shifts towards export-orientation in Latin America, Diaz-Alejandro concludes that political repression and outward-orientation were not closely related (1983, pp. 37–44; cf. Hirschman, 1981, pp. 114–115). He suggests that the most vicious market-authoritarian episodes in Latin America originated in unhinged macroeconomic conditions, which could have been avoided through sounder macroeconomic and growth-oriented policies (ibid., p. 49).

In developing countries shifting towards democracy, the moderation of urban wage demands may be crucial to exporting success and long-run prosperity. To avoid an often-brutal free market outcome, one strategy here would be twofold. Firstly, the priority for growth would be to raise employment levels rather than real wages. Secondly, the state would act as mediator between capital and labour, dividing between them the benefits of rising output and productivity, and ensuring the competitiveness of industry. Such a corporatist outcome, however, would be difficult to achieve in conflict-ridden societies.

Redistribution and growth?
Three sets of growth strategies can be distinguished for developing countries. One can be termed the 'grow now, redistribute later' approach, relying on 'trickle-down' effects to ensure that poor people will benefit in the long run. The other extreme can be termed 'redistribute now, grow later', while the third option is somewhere between the two – a 'redistribute and grow' approach.

The first option is suspect at best. The 'growth-first' call is often used to justify a range of repressive and vicious economic practices, trickle-down effects may take ages to materialise, the strategy may not be efficient (failing, for example, to invest adequately in human capital and skills), and can be viewed as highly unjust (cf. Fields, 1980, ch. 5). Vague promises of benefits in generations to come are not politically or morally attractive to deprived and marginalised people.

The second and third options have a great deal more in their favour. To begin with, it is often argued that there is a relation between the degree of equality at the start of a growth-period and the trend of equality during growth. Most countries which have grown rapidly and equitably began their growth-phases with a relatively even distribution of assets (physical and human) and income – for example, Taiwan, the Republic of Korea, Costa Rica, and Yugoslavia for quite some time during the 1950s and 1960s

(Bergsman, 1979). By contrast, many which grew fast but began with high levels of inequality – for example, Brazil, the Philippines – experienced rising inequality over long periods (Fields, 1980, pp. 210–228; T. Moll, 1990, pp. 18–23). In cases like the latter, owners of assets appear to benefit the most from growth, and it is difficult to modify income flows substantially using instruments like government spending, taxes and labour market policies (Morawetz, 1980, p. 353). It is thus often concluded that equitable growth requires a 'redistribute first, grow later' strategy.

Along these lines, Griffin and James (1979, 1981) suggest that redistributive attempts should immediately restructure the system of socio-political relations in society, otherwise such attempts are likely to be ineffective in the long run. They argue that the systems of asset distribution (they refer mainly to land), income distribution (returns from assets, mainly wages and social security payments) and the structure of demand need to be changed together, otherwise a change in one may well be cancelled out by compensating changes in the others (1981, ch. 2). Typically, rises in nominal wages on their own may simply raise spending on (price-inelastic) food and hence food prices and the income of large landowners, thus negating the original wage rises and doing little for the income distribution.

Griffin and James claim that market systems are self-regulating, such that marginal shifts in income are unlikely to have substantial long-run effects (1979, p. 249). The simulations of Adelman, Morris and Robinson (1976, pp. 570–575), for example, imply for post-war Korea that quite large changes in the distribution of incremental income would have small long-run effects on the income shares of poor people.[8] According to this approach, it is essential to carry out systematic restructuring attempts across a broad economic front immediately a new government takes power. Since major redistributional attempts involving sharp changes in the distribution of assets and incomes require radical social change and imply temporary economic dislocations, Griffin and James recommend the use of various state controls to help get through the transitional period – for example, distributing (some) food to poor people, direct controls over foreign exchange and some prices, and so on (1981, ch. 4).

This version of the 'redistribute first, grow later' approach suggests that radical results need immediate radical interventions, and that efforts at reformism which do not attempt to restructure social and economic relations sharply are likely to be ineffective. The cases of revolutionary China and Cuba, and Chile in the early 1970s, are discussed in this regard, in decreasing order of effectiveness (Griffin and James, 1981, ch. 7). There are a number of problems with the Griffin–James approach, however. Firstly, they consider a limited range of countries, and their 'successful' cases are all at fairly low levels of development. They do not show that a more gradual approach is generally ineffective (demonstrating this only in a few cases), nor is it clear that their radical strategy can work in middle-income economies with small agricultural sectors. Secondly, they do not consider the long-term growth–

redistribution relation; despite some vigorous defences, the growth records of Cuba and China in the decade or more after redistribution, for example, were poor.

The crucial problem with the 'redistribute now, grow later' approach is that the growth–equity tradeoff may be strong 'if the method of redistribution chosen carries within it the seeds of a low long-run investment rate, a slow rate of increase in productivity, or some other type of direct damage to growth prospects' (Morawetz, 1980, p. 353), as appears to have been the case in Sri Lanka (high consumption subsidies reducing investment and distorting production incentives) and Cuba (incentive and productivity problems to do with state ownership). The dismal long-run records of many socialist countries suggest that many forms of large-scale public ownership carry within them the seeds of failure. Further, one crucial asset – education – can only be redistributed slowly and with difficulty.

By contrast to the above approach are various 'redistribute and grow' options. According to Chenery et al. (1974), political situations in developing countries do not allow radical income redistributions (nor would they be effective); instead, marginal increments to income should be channelled to poor people, to be used as efficiently as possible. Similar views are advanced by Ascher (1984). He argues that the distributional situation in developing countries is subtle and flexible. Many radical politicians achieved little, despite following a Griffin–James type of all-out approach, while some moderate reformers achieved a great deal, despite proceeding by means of low-key reforms.

Ascher suggests that political processes, alliances and struggles are complex, with lots of governments having abundant scope for manoeuvre if they wish, and discusses several post-war South American cases – Peru, Chile and Argentina – in these terms. Typically, he claims that Velasco's radical military reformism in Peru after 1968 achieved more of its objectives than Allende's socialist transformation of Chile after 1970, simply because measures used were more cunningly chosen and better political alliances were achieved in the former case. Velasco's approach was less aggregated, using more subtle and precise policy levers, while his measures were slow and adjustable and did not make clear the limits of redistribution from the start, thus helping to disorganise the middle classes (1984, pp. 294–295). Along similar lines, Sheahan (1987, pp. 315–316) argues that 'middle road' market systems in Latin America have done more for poor people in the long run than have more radical reformists, in large part because their limited reform packages were more practical and achievable than radical programmes, and avoided the dangers of economic breakdown. It is curious to note, however, that reformist regimes in Latin America have not been notable political successes. In many cases they were politically unpopular, lacking support from the right but being unable to consolidate support from the working classes, thus some of the efforts made were not sustained in the long run (Ascher, 1984, ch. 10).

It is difficult to generalise about these issues. Ascher shows that moderate and gradual reformism, carried out by cunning political strategists, can have important effects on poverty and even on the distribution of assets and income, while in some cases he discusses, radicals failed to carry out their programmes in the long run and suffered from more immediate failures than the reformists. Griffin and James demonstrate that certain large-scale redistributional ends require systematic and complementary policies, may entail direct controls of various kinds to carry the measures through, and may imply significant transitional losses. The chief problem is that it is difficult to take from the rich except by decisive asset-expropriating strategies, entailing higher short-run and sometimes long-run costs. Perhaps the crucial question concerns the extent to which assertive redistributional programmes can be implemented without the sharp and inefficient expansion of state economic power in society.

Conclusion

Many would-be redistributive packages discussed above provide warnings rather than models – they demonstrate rather well what redistributors in countries like South Africa should avoid, but often fail to suggest exactly what can be done. Their example is mostly negative but valuable all the same, in part because many failures have been due to similar patterns of simplistic or incompetent policymaking. There are also lessons to be learned from successful 'reformist' regimes, most importantly that packages of marginal but systematic reforms will not transform society quickly but can help to eliminate poverty and redistribute assets towards poor people in the long term.

Despite the complexity of the material covered above, two general hypotheses about the redistribution–growth relation can be advanced. The first concerns the costs of asset and income redistribution. Many kinds of redistribution associated with a 'redistribute and grow' strategy – land reforms, higher educational spending on poor people, higher spending on children, moderate tax reforms – have low growth costs, if any, and may be productive in the long run (see the previous chapter in this volume). By contrast, some more radical measures – which destabilise macroeconomic balance or involve the large-scale redistribution of non-land assets – tend to have much higher costs in the short and the long run, and may entail permanently slower growth. It is also clear that the costs of many mild reforms may be predictably low, while the costs of radical restructuring can be high and unpredictable.

Some of the reasons for this are obvious. Mild reforms often involve little change in socio-economic relations: people continue doing things much as before, under slightly different – and hopefully more favourable – conditions. Providing food for schoolchildren does not need much of an organisational initiative and should have limited macroeconomic effects. By contrast, radical reforms involve sharp changes in social relations, at various levels of society, all at the same time. Nationalising firms might involve new managers moving in without proper training, large-scale land reforms might involve people lacking agricultural experience moving onto the land, while such efforts might need to be complemented by some state distribution of food and other items. Ascher (1984, p. 317) stresses that the technical problems of calibrating such 'all out' income redistribution programmes can be awesome, leading to the possibility of devastating economic dislocations.

The second hypothesis concerns the level of development of society. The more advanced the economy, the higher the costs of radical restructuring are likely to be, because of problems relating to information and the coordination of economic activity. In simple agriculture-based economies, restructuring may well be quite straightforward: give peasants the land (which they have been working anyway), provide some state services (e.g. agricultural extension and marketing work), and wait for output and productivity to rise. By contrast, in more developed economies like that of South Africa, the issues are far more complex. It is much more difficult to nationalise a large mine than to reform large *latifundia* efficiently. In the latter case, the division of labour will be less advanced and economies of scale are likely to be small, while in the former there are many skills which come with the mine managers, the loss of which would be considerable, while economies of scale are much larger. Part of the problem in richer economies characterised by some flexibility and resource mobility is that direct controls do not work easily, as they can be evaded by markets of various kinds. Likewise, more advanced economies tend to have stronger linkages to the international economy and are more subject to economic opposition in the form of money and human capital flight, loss of access to international capital and goods markets, and so on.

On a strategic note, a major difficulty with redistributive programmes is that they tend not to be politically viable in the long run. Where redistributive states wish to retain power, two strategic issues come to the fore. The first concerns the issue of transition costs: other things being equal, the more decisive the redistribution of income, the higher the likely costs of transition. For redistributors, this implies policies of political restraint, reducing excessive expectations. As Lehmann puts it, based on his analysis of the Allende period, 'Political forces seeking to undertake a redistribution of income could learn this one lesson from the Chilean experience: to be on the safe side, plan for austerity, not for a consumption boom' in the first year or two of the new regime (1978, p. 113), as a rapid expansion of demand might well nullify the whole effort (Seers, 1981; Morawetz, 1980, p. 358). Pedraza-Bailey (1982, p. 47) in fact argues that the Popular Unity government should have tried to persuade the workers to accept lower real wages in 1970–1, to enable the Allende regime to survive the hard times of socialist transition.

The second strategic point is that redistributive states should produce packages of policies, some with short-run effects, others which pay off in the long run. Immediate gains like abundant urban site-and-service schemes or meals for rural schoolchildren can yield useful political returns, even where real wages and employment levels are hardly affected. In the medium run, lower barriers to entry and efforts to push large firms into raising linkages with small ones might help, while in the long run issues of skills, education and export-strategies are paramount. Judicious selection of sets of policies gradually to improve the living conditions of the poor can be the most viable politically – together with vigorous publicity about state achievements in such areas! One extreme to be avoided is sudden, drastic rises in worker living standards: rarely do they have corresponding political payoffs, they create expectations for more such rises, which are rarely possible, they lead to reduced support when (as often happens) they must later be partly reversed, and they do little for very poor people.

3

A tax strategy for redistribution

LIEB J. LOOTS

This chapter starts off from the premise that 'redistribution' (reducing poverty and inequality) is a desirable policy objective and worthy of serious consideration by economists. Moreover, any concern with the sustainability of a programme of redistribution must necessarily give consideration to the relationship between redistribution and growth. This discussion of tax policy in South Africa is no exception.

Economists have long adhered to two fundamental concepts of fairness: horizontal equity and vertical equity. These principles could be seen as dealing with substantive fairness. However, while not underestimating the importance of these two principles, I argue in this chapter that we should be especially concerned with perceived fairness.

The concern with perceived fairness makes particular sense in the context of my primary concern in this chapter, that of an efficient tax structure. The focus on efficiency reflects the view that the overall redistributive effect of the government's fiscal policies is more dependent on the expenditure side than on the tax side of the budget.

Redistribution is a function of the whole fiscal system. The perceived fairness of the tax system obviously depends on the vantage point of the individual or interest group concerned. Equity and justice in the design of tax systems are complex. The answers to such questions will vary with the particular notion of justice that is chosen. Nevertheless, it is likely that 'perceived fairness' in a newly democratised South Africa will be strongly influenced by the (perceived) redistributive characteristics of the fiscal system as a whole and not just the tax structure.

While the concern with redistribution thus applies to the fiscal programme as a whole, the efficiency of the tax system itself can be severely undermined if it is perceived as unfair. The poll tax in Britain and township rates in South Africa are just two of the most notable current examples. The large degree of income tax avoidance in many countries and a tax morality which undermines voluntary compliance, are too well known to be ignored. The perception that the tax system, or a particular tax, is not fair, would be an important contributing factor in many of these cases. Efficiency demands that attention be given to perceived fairness.

It is necessary, therefore, that 'both' sides of the redistributive divide should perceive the tax system as fair. On the one hand it is necessary to increase the likelihood of more voluntary compliance with the tax laws and minimise the extent of tax avoidance. On the other hand it is necessary for the majority of the electorate to perceive the tax structure as fair enough so as not to push for taxes which may have a harmful effect on the economy. 'Fairness' thus remains an important prerequisite if we want to maximise state revenue through an efficient tax structure.

In short, I argue in this chapter that the main task of policy on the revenue side is to construct a tax system which is efficient in raising revenue on a sustainable basis. This in turn determines the degree of redistribution which can be obtained on the expenditure side of the budget. If the fiscal system is perceived as fair it is more likely that tax avoidance can be prevented and voluntary compliance adhered to.

Not only must the overall rate of taxation in the economy be sustainable from year to year, but it is also necessary that the tax system promotes growth, or at least does not hamper it, in order to be able to increase government revenue as a proportion of GDP. Only then will it be possible for a programme of redistribution to be sustained and indeed extended. This necessitates that fiscal policies, and tax policies specifically, give due weight to the encouragement of growth. This is discussed in the latter part of this chapter.

Thus, a progressive and sustainable strategy of redistribution demands a tax structure which is efficient in raising revenue, something which is only possible if the tax system is perceived as fair. A sustainable strategy of redistribution also requires that further significant increases in the overall tax level in the economy be considered only in the context of rising per capita incomes. The most important determinant of the rate at which this can occur, is the growth rate of the economy. Sustainable and extendable redistribution thus also necessitates a tax system which can promote economic growth.

TAX STRUCTURE

The first issue to consider regarding the efficiency of the tax system, is the tax structure, including both the share of government revenue in GDP and the composition of government revenue. These will be discussed in turn.

Overall tax level

The share of government revenue is important as there is a strongly held opinion amongst most tax analysts that too high a government share of GDP may have negative allocative and growth implications for the economy. What 'too high' might be is of course debatable and I shall not attempt a specification of such an optimal level. However, an international comparison of government revenue levels provides an indication of the appropriate order of magnitude for a country with South Africa's level of development and per capita income.

Table 3.1 places South Africa among the middle-income countries in terms of the share of total tax revenue in GDP in the early 1980s.

Table 3.1.   Share of tax revenue in gross domestic product: selected countries

	1980/1	1987
Industrial countries:		
Ireland	34	40
Germany	38	38
United Kingdom	35	38
Greece	29	37
Italy	30	36
Spain	24	33
Portugal	29	31
United States	30	30
Japan	25	30
Unweighted mean, OECD countries	35	39
Developing middle-income countries:		
Brazil	23	
South Africa	20	27
Turkey	22	24
Singapore	18	
Argentina	19	
Developing low-income countries:		
Zimbabwe	24	
Indonesia	22	
Zaire	18	
India	16	

Source: Margo Commission Report (1987) and Owens (1990), p. 33.

The shares in Table 3.1 suggest that it may be possible for a middle- or lower-income country to increase its tax revenue to between 20 per cent and 30 per cent of GDP, but that tax revenue above that and particularly shares above 35 per cent of GDP may well be the preserve of countries with a high per capita GDP. By 1990, South Africa had already pushed its total government revenue up to about 30 per cent of GDP (*Statistical/Economic Review 1990/91*). This suggests that further increases in government revenue from taxation may not only be difficult to introduce without allocative and growth costs, but may well be dependent on increases in per capita GDP, something South Africa, in contrast to all other countries with tax shares higher than itself, was not able to achieve during the 1980s.

Together, the OECD countries, in spite of their positive GDP growth rates, increased the tax level by only 4 percentage points over the period 1980–7, after which the tax ratio stabilised, and in some cases started decreasing moderately towards the end of the decade (Owens, 1990). This may serve as a caution to policymakers in South Africa not to increase the tax level too rapidly without careful analysis of its possible effects on the economy. At the very least, it suggests that the maximum increase in the tax level could be between 0,5 percentage point of GDP per year (roughly the OECD average for 1980–7) and 1,0 percentage point of GDP per year (roughly the South African average for 1980–90) – given that other factors, such as a positive growth rate, are favourable.

One rationale in support of such a proposition has to do with the nature of much of government expenditure. Even if it will eventually lead to greater productivity – for example, as a result of spending more on education – it will only happen over a relatively long period of time, or only occur in relatively small increases per year. Where this kind of 'social investment' has been inadequate or ineffective in the past, as is the case in South Africa, this gestation period is bound to be even longer or more gradual. In the interim, the much faster increase in 'investment' expenditure, in contrast with the increase in the stream of benefits resulting from it, might well create enough instability in the economy to seriously undermine the very objectives which the rapid tax-level increases were intended to achieve. In other words, given the legacy of wasteful apartheid expenditure, and even assuming that the South African tax level has not yet reached some optimal level, there is a case to be made for a very gradual, rather than a rapid, increase in the tax share of GDP.

Ultimately public spending is limited by the ability of the public sector to transfer to itself resources from the private sector through taxes (and less importantly from charges) on current economic activities, or to issue public debt secured by taxes on future economic activities. If the deficit is to be contained within acceptable limits and if the tax level can only be increased gradually, it follows that the potential increase in total government expenditure will be determined largely by the increase in GDP.

It can be deduced, therefore, that tax reform in South Africa, while aimed at gradually increasing the overall tax level, should primarily be concerned with the equity and efficiency aspects of the tax system. The tax mix, or tax structure, may consequently be of much greater importance for tax policy, at least over the short term, than the level of taxation in the economy.

Tax structure in South Africa
South Africa underwent some significant changes in its tax structure between 1975 and 1989, as Table 3.2 shows.

In broad relative terms there has been a shift away from direct taxes towards indirect taxes, although the former slightly increased their share in terms of GDP. This has been brought about mainly by the increased share of GDP collected in the form of GST.

Within the structure of direct taxes there has been a significant reduction

Table 3.2.   Shares of various sources of government revenue

Classification of source	1975/6 % of GDP	1975/6 % of total rev.	1980/1 % of GDP	1980/1 % of total rev.	1989/90 % of GDP	1989/90 % of total rev.	OECD 1980 % of total rev.	OECD 1988 %of total rev.
Individuals	–	–	3,3	13,7	8,0	27,0	31	29
Companies	–	–	3,8	15,8	4,6	15,7	6	7
Gold mines	–	–	4,4	18,3	0,4	1,5		
Other mines	–	–	0,3	1,4	0,6	1,9		
Non–residents' share tax	–	–	0,5	2,0	0,2	0,6		
Direct taxes	12,4	53,2	12,4	51,2	13,8	46,7	37	36
Customs + Excise	–	–	2,3	9,7	3,7	12,5	10	10
Sales tax	–	–	2,6	10,8	6,9	23,5	13	16
Local/reg. govt.	2,9	12,4	3,0	12,4	3,6	12,2		
Other taxes	–	–	0,6	2,3	0,6	1,9	6	4
Indirect taxes	6,7	28,8	8,5	35,5	14,8	50,1	29	30
Social security	–	–	–	–	–	–	24	24
Miscellaneous	4,2	18,0	3,2	13,3	0,9	3,1	10	10
Total revenue	23,3	100,0	24,0	100,0	29,5	100,0	100	100

Sources: Calculations based on Margo Commission Report (1987); *Statistical Economic Review 1990/1*; and Owens (1990).

in taxes on gold-mine incomes. This has been more than compensated for by the increase (in real and relative terms) in personal income tax. Non-mining company income tax in South Africa, while increasing slightly as a proportion of GDP, maintained roughly its share of total tax revenue. However, if mining is added, as is the case in other countries, the share of company income tax drops quite significantly (Table 3.2). It fell from 8,5 per cent of GDP and 35,5 per cent of total tax revenue to 5,6 per cent and 19,1 per cent respectively. This contributed to the shift towards indirect taxes.

While the tax structure has therefore become less progressive overall, the test of fairness ('vertical equity' in economic jargon) should apply to each tax individually and not necessarily to the tax system as a whole. Whatever the exact progressivity of a particular tax might be, however, it may not be possible to increase the revenue capacity of the tax system without, at the same time, making the whole tax system less progressive than before.

For example, once all the direct taxes, which can be more progressive than indirect taxes, have been introduced, their bases extended to the maximum and their rates raised to the maximum levels, the only way in which the tax capacity of the economy can be extended is through the introduction of indirect taxes. Moreover, in reality the attainment of such an optimal situation with respect to direct, progressive taxes is hardly ever possible and the need therefore remains to capture untapped tax potential which is lost through the direct tax net.

All countries have a tax system consisting of a whole range of direct and indirect taxes. A goal with tax policy should be to develop a balanced tax system, rather than maximum progressivity for its own sake. High top-income tax rates without less progressive indirect taxes could therefore not only fail to guarantee effective (or realisable) progressivity, but might also reduce the total revenue which could be raised, particularly from the wealthy for redistribution on the expenditure side.

The relevance of the last point to the questions of equity (fairness) and efficiency, is that this may be an instance where both efficiency and equity could suffer as a result of a too rapidly rising tax gradient (how quickly tax rates increase as incomes increase). This gives an incentive to high-income salary earners to avoid tax, or for companies to find non-taxable ways of remunerating their high-salaried workers. Middle-income salary earners thus carry a relatively heavier tax burden than other taxpayers with the same or even higher incomes. Not only does equity suffer as a result, but also efficiency. Less-than-optimal tax revenue could be the result.

The belief that this is not just a theoretical possibility but a real likelihood, has led to an international trend towards lowering rates. The lowering of top rates is reflected in Table 3.3.

Table 3.3.   Top and first positive rates of the central government personal income tax: 1986 and 1990

Country	Top rates[a]		Country	First positive rates[a]	
	1986	1990		1986	1990
Sweden[b]	50	20	United Kingdom	29	25
United States	50	28	Germany	22	19
United Kingdom	60	40	Italy	12	10
Japan	70	50	Japan	10,5	10
Greece	63	50	Turkey	25	25
Italy	62	50	United States	11	15
Spain	66	56	Greece	10	18
Germany	56	53	Sweden	4	20
Turkey	50	50	Spain	8	25
Unweighted mean of all OECD countries	54	43		15	17
South Africa	50	44	South Africa	–	16

Notes: [a] 'First positive rate' refers to the tax rate applicable to a tax payer when he/she first starts paying income tax. 'Top rate' refers to the highest tax rate applicable to any additional income earned by taxpayers in the highest income bracket. [b] Sweden 1991.
Source: Owens (1990), p. 42.

Virtually all OECD countries have, between 1986 and 1990, reduced their top personal income tax rates. The unweighted mean fell from 54 to 43 per cent of taxable income. A similar trend, of almost exactly the same average dimensions, can be observed among developing countries (OECD, 1990b). However, this did not result in a significant reduction in the share of personal income tax in total tax revenue. The two most likely reasons for this are the reduction of the tax avoidance incentive as a result of the lowering of top rates and the (related) removal or limitation of tax reliefs (Owens, 1990).

The overall conclusion is thus that the widespread reforms of the personal income tax structure, and particularly the strong trend towards the reduction of top rates, have not significantly reduced the overall progressivity of the tax structure. It has improved, however, the efficiency of personal income tax by making it more simple (thus reducing compliance costs), more equitable (through the removal of selective tax relief) and more neutral (through making it less likely that the personal tax system will influence people's decisions). Such tax reform thus moves closer to an optimal balance between equity and efficiency.

TAX POLICY AND REDISTRIBUTION

I have already argued that the challenge of tax policy is to design a tax structure which is efficient in raising revenue and perceived to be fair, and then spend the revenue in a way which can achieve sustainable redistribution. The redistributive potential of the tax system is more fully explored in this section.

Taxation of income

The distribution of income in South Africa shows a substantial degree of inequality. In South Africa, the legacy of apartheid is one of the most unequal distributions of income of any country for which statistics are available. This high degree of inequality is the result of both the unequal investment in labour skills or ability (human capital) and of the legal, social and demographic forces which determine relative wages and salaries. It is therefore certain that distributional concerns will continue to be a vital factor in politics and policy determination.

It is postulated, therefore, that in a post-apartheid and democratic South Africa, public expenditures on social investment (in human capital), benefits-in-kind (including merit goods) and transfer payments will become an important part of the 'social wage' (improvements in the quality of life of workers provided to them by the state). The benefits of public expenditures will continue to play an important political role in the post-apartheid era.

Most economists agree that there is a limit to the amount of redistribution that can take place through the tax system. In crude terms, it is argued that taxes cannot make poor people rich. If our main concern is with poverty as such, with the waste and misuse of human resources which it produces, remedies must come primarily through the expenditure side of the budget.

This could be done either by direct public provision of such services as housing, medical care, and education, or by simple transfers of income, or through employment-creating policies.

It is in this context that I wish to argue that the tax system, while perceived to be fair, must have as primary objective the maximisation of tax revenues in order to meet the 'social wage' commitments on the expenditure side of the budget that are necessitated by political, moral and indeed economic imperatives.

Some indication of the distribution of income before and after personal income tax can be gleaned from Table 3.4, which was estimated on the basis of such limited information as could be obtained.

Table 3.4.   Redistributive effect of income tax, South Africa 1984/5

Quartile	Total income before ind. tax		Total individ. income tax		Income after	
	Rm	%	Rm	%	Rm	%
0–25	1 775	2,5	0,0	0,0	1 775	2,8
25–75	24 331	34,8	0,0	0,0	24 331	38,9
75–100	43 895	62,7	7 377	100,0	36 519	58,3
Total	70 000	100,0	7 377	100,0	62 625	100,0

Source: Own calculations. See Loots (1991), Table 3.1.

The estimates, while they need to be treated with circumspection, suggest that it is likely that only 25 per cent of the economically active population earn about 63 per cent of income and pay virtually all of individual income tax. This must clearly have a redistributive effect on income shares received by individuals. The top 25 per cent, whose share of income before tax fell from 63 per cent to 58 per cent after income tax, lost out to the middle group, whose share rose from 35 per cent to 39 per cent.

While the imposition of a progressive income-tax structure has reduced the extreme concentration of personal income, the effect has not been

Table 3.5.   Income tax paid by top 25 per cent of income earners

Percentiles	Taxable income before tax %	Income tax paid %	Income after tax tax %	Average rate %
76–80	3,4	0,03	3,80	0,01
81–85	10,2	1,30	11,25	2,20
86–90	13,3	5,84	14,18	7,59
91–95	26,2	21,94	26,70	14,48
96–100	46,9	70,89	44,07	26,14
Total	100,0	100,00	100,00	10,54

Source: Own calculations. See Loots (1991).

dramatic, hardly changing the position of the lowest quartile of the economically active. This is the inevitable result of the very skewed distribution of
income and the extremely narrow tax base resulting from it. It also indicates
the limited possibility of significantly increasing the personal income-tax
base in the near future.

This is brought out even more startlingly by Table 3.5 which gives similar
percentages for the top 25 per cent of income-tax payers only. The table
suggests that such redistribution as is achieved through personal income tax,
is mostly from the top 5 per cent of income-tax payers to people in the 25–75
per cent category. In spite of the fact that the top 5 per cent pay 71 per cent
of all income tax, their share of income is only reduced from 47 per cent to
44 per cent as a result of the tax. While this group is already subject to an
average tax rate of 26 per cent (39 per cent in the case of the top 1 per cent,
the top marginal rate being 50 per cent), there appear to be efficiency
constraints on increasing the income-tax rates in the higher-income brackets.
It therefore seems highly unlikely that personal income tax can be used as a
significant redistributive mechanism in the future. This is in line with the
current thinking of most tax experts in the world.

Even if personal income tax cannot be used for effective redistribution, it
should be subject to consideration for tax reform. Serious consideration ought
to be given to making the tax more efficient. The strong international trend
in this direction has already been noted. South Africa has started on the road
of tax reform by, for example, reducing the top marginal tax rate from 50 per
cent to 44 per cent. Broadening of the tax base has already begun, through
taxation of fringe benefits and the imposition of ceilings on deductions from
taxable income. Further tax reform in this area is desirable.

Widening the income-tax base takes the form of either abolishing or
limiting (usually by ceilings) tax reliefs for specific expenditures (typically
on home ownership, other interest payments and business expenses) or
bringing new forms of income-tax into the tax base or widening the definition
of such taxable income (typically fringe benefits and capital gains). If this
were to be done in South Africa, income-tax revenue would probably be
increased enough to compensate for the lowering of the top rate. A rough
estimate suggests that reducing the top rate to 40 per cent with a maximum
income tax of 30 per cent of income would result in a revenue loss of no more
than about 4 per cent of personal income tax.

While such rate changes, if viewed in isolation, would appear to reduce
the progressivity of income-tax schedules, it is likely that this loss of
progressivity would be partially, if not totally, offset by base-broadening or
by increases in tax thresholds. (In South Africa the tax threshold was
increased by about R4000, or 69 per cent of its former level, in 1990.) To the
extent that it would reduce the incentive for tax avoidance, such changes
would further restore or maintain the progressivity of income tax. As such
changes to income-rate schedules are dictated rather by economic efficiency
and horizontal equity considerations than by vertical equity, it becomes an

empirical matter to what extent and in what manner they should be introduced. Tax policy research in this area is thus necessary.

A study of tax reform in Jamaica's personal income tax found that evasion and avoidance all but negated the progressivity of the statutory rate structure, leading to the reform of the tax system. It now appears that the combination of a higher standard deduction, a broadened base, and a lower flat rate has improved the administration and increased the progressivity of the tax system. Revenues from income taxes were 18 per cent higher in the 12-month period after the introduction of the reform.

There appears to be some potential for the widening of South Africa's income-tax base. Base-broadening should reduce or eliminate tax expenditures available only to certain categories of taxpayer, and those more easily exploitable by high-income earners.

Capital gains tax

The wealthy often receive income in the form of a capital gain. For reasons of equity, most developed and many developing countries have a capital gains tax in one form or another. It is a complex issue, but one which needs to be given serious consideration for the reason of perceived fairness already discussed.

The traditional concept of income, which is reflected in South Africa's tax legislation, draws a distinction between capital and income, and only regards gains in the latter as taxable. A more modern approach to the problem includes in the concept of income all accretions to the taxpayer's economic power, i.e. his power, whether exercised or not, to consume goods and services. According to this comprehensive approach, it is not necessary to distinguish between the different causes of an increase in economic power. It is therefore irrelevant whether the gain results from work effort, gifts, capital gains or some other windfall. The only requirement is that it must apply to realised gains.

There are many arguments in favour of and against the imposition of a capital gains tax. The Margo Commission concluded that the costs outweighed the gains and rejected it. A minority recommendation, however, was in favour of the principle of introducing a capital gains tax. It reaffirmed the majority report of the Franzsen Commission on this issue, believing that equity should be the deciding factor.

Most developed and many less-developed countries have opted for a capital gains tax on grounds of equity. These decisions were taken even though the fiscal authorities concerned were well aware of the complexities and administrative difficulties that have to be faced in applying this tax in practice.

The minority recommendation further argued that because wealthy persons own more capital assets than the less well-to-do, it is obvious that more capital gains will accrue to the former. Hence the exemption of capital gains promotes an unequal distribution of the tax burden and erodes the progressivity of the income tax system. Studies undertaken by the Brookings Institution indicate that in the United States richer people derive a relatively greater proportion of their 'economic power', i.e. their ability to pay, from capital gains, which also enable them to effect income switching. Critics of a capital gains tax emphasise its low yield. The Irish Tax Commission countered this argument as follows: 'On the contrary, we believe that a major reason for charging capital gains to tax is to prevent avoidance of income tax by switching income gains into a form in which they are regarded as capital gains. This is not only necessary for reasons of equity, as not all taxpayers are able to effect this kind of switch; it is also necessary for reasons of efficiency to prevent investment distortion. Furthermore, in so far as the presence of a capital gains tax deters such switches, it will serve to protect the yield of income tax. Thus, even on the narrow criterion of revenue yield, its contribution will be more than is apparent from looking at the yield of capital gains tax in isolation.' (First Report, 1982, p. 201)

A strong case thus exists, in the South African situation, to give serious consideration to the minority recommendation which expressed support for the version of a capital gains tax that would: be at a low rate and indexed for inflation; differentiate between short-term and long-term gains; be confined to dealings in fixed property and securities; be effective from a fixed date; allow for capital losses; and amend the definition of 'capital and income' in order to make it clear that the Commissioner of Inland Revenue would not have the option of imposing either capital gains tax or tax at ordinary rates.

Minimum business tax
Another aspect which deserves consideration for reasons of broadening the income-tax base and adding to the perceived fairness of the tax system is to place limits on the maximum number of deductions which can be claimed against income or tax in any one year, thus effectively imposing a minimum tax. Such a minimum income tax should apply to both companies and individuals, particularly those able to deduct excessive expenditures against revenue.

In the specific case of companies and other businesses, a minimum tax could also provide a corporate tax base that would be immune to some of the shortcomings of the income tax. These are that the profits tax base is too small (typically no more than about 20 per cent of GNP), too volatile, too easy to manipulate and too difficult to measure (especially in times of inflation and with respect to inventories and depreciation). Businesses have been able in the past to combine the available deductions, introduced to act as incentives for specific activities, in a way that eliminated their tax liability.

In addition, use of a profits base tends to penalise efficient firms, allowing inefficient firms to pay no taxes if they earn no profits, even if they have made huge demands on the infrastructure and other communal resources. In other words, the profits base gives too little weight to the benefit principle, which, however valid for individuals (particularly wage and salary earners), is of doubtful relevance to companies.

Various possibilities exist in designing a minimum tax. For example, it can be expressed as a portion of taxable income before the subtraction of the concessional deductions; or it can be calculated as a percentage of the sum of the deductions themselves. Another possibility which warrants further investigation is to rest the minimum tax on a value-added base.

That base, essentially consisting of the sum of all incomes generated in a business less an allowance for gross investment, could form a base for a minimum tax, even if a major tax is not levied on that base. The base for such a tax is large, over 80 per cent of GDP. It can thus be introduced at a very low rate, so limiting distortionary effects. For example, assume that businesses manage to avoid paying on average 10 per cent of income tax. Company tax is currently about 5 per cent of GDP but should, under this assumption, be 5,5 per cent of GDP. The minimum tax, based on the additive value-added tax base, should thus be constructed to raise 0,5 per cent of GDP. With the tax base 80 per cent of GDP, a rate of 0,7 per cent will be enough to raise the required revenue.

The introduction of a simplified version of a minimum tax based on value added and using the information already generated by VAT, would also give the tax authorities experience in this type of tax which could inform future tax-reform considerations. It must be kept in mind, though, that such a tax would be a minimum tax only, providing a threshold below which income tax cannot fall. In other words, the minimum tax falls away as the income tax becomes positive and approaches the minimum tax level. It therefore would only penalise inefficient firms.

REDISTRIBUTION OF WEALTH

The unequal distribution of wealth in South Africa is well known and receives constant political attention. According to the studies of McGrath (1983), the ownership of private wealth is very concentrated in South Africa when compared with leading countries in the developed Western world. He indicates that the top 5 per cent of wealth-owners account for 88 per cent of personally owned wealth, compared with 54 per cent in Great Britain, 34 per cent in West Germany and 44 per cent in the United States. A tax system which does not address this inequality will be perceived as unfair by the majority of the population. It is thus necessary, in the interest of efficiency, that wealth be taxed in some form or another.

It has been pointed out that capital as such contributes to a person's ability to pay taxes, and consequently offers a further potential base for levying tax. However, it has been found that the revenue yield of capital taxes tends to be relatively small and that it 'is unlikely to be the dominant consideration in the introduction or retention of a capital tax' and that 'the main rationale for taxing capital relates to social considerations' (OECD, 1979).

More important than the revenue considerations is the concern in South Africa with the inequalities which were shaped, at least partially, by the apartheid system. The main rationale for taxing wealth relates to social considerations, i.e. considerations of equity between persons within society. This concern is not adequately addressed by the taxes to which capital is currently subject, i.e. an estate duty, a donations tax and local-authority land taxes. It is for this reason that some other potential capital taxes are considered.

A balanced and more efficient tax system will have a progressive tax pyramid, i.e. flat-rate consumption taxes at the bottom, progressive income taxes in the middle, and capital taxes (as well as luxury consumption taxes), which affect only a few, at the top.

Wealth tax

Two of the arguments raised against a wealth tax are that it creates substantial administrative complications and is costly to administer, and that it penalises saving and may act as a disincentive for taxpayers to save.

The administrative and cost problems associated with a wealth tax have been documented and must be taken seriously. Moreover, if the rate is high in order to raise more revenue or make a more effective impact on the distribution of wealth, capital tends to migrate to another tax jurisdiction where a lesser burden is imposed.

The determination of the tax base raises questions about the inclusion of such things as household effects, personal effects and jewellery, pension rights, life assurance policies, works of art, owner-occupied houses and patent rights, copyright and goodwill. The valuation of assets poses a serious problem to the introduction of a net wealth tax. Some of these problem assets are unquoted shares, unincorporated businesses, agricultural land, usufructuary rights and other immoveable property.

Another problem with an annual net wealth tax is the effect it will have on the market prices of assets. If someone bought an asset many years ago when the market value was low and found its value increasing faster than the current income of the owner, a net wealth tax could create serious cash-flow problems for the owner.

It is worth taking note of the Margo Commission's mention of the fact that both the Carter Commission (Canada, 1966) and the Asprey Committee (Australia, 1975) considered the possibility of a net wealth tax, but rejected it. The Irish Commission (1982) came to the conclusion that, provided income – including realised capital gains and gifts and inheritances – is charged to tax on a comprehensive basis at a single rate and dissavings are charged to a direct expenditure tax at progressive rates, the case for a general tax on capital is weak. That commission accordingly recommended that an annual wealth tax should not be introduced.

Capital transfer tax

Following the recommendation of the Irish Commission that the taxation of capital through the imposition of comprehensive taxation of gifts and inheritances should be imposed, our attention turns to the capital transfer tax. Death duties and donations are indeed transfers of capital.

Capital transfer taxes are found in most OECD countries (Margo, 1987). South Africa already has death or estate duties and associated gift taxes. These taxes are not integrated, though, and are also so low as not to have any marked effect on the concentration of wealth.

Consideration ought therefore be given to a single capital transfer tax to be imposed on dispositions of property for no or for inadequate remuneration. Special attention must also be given to the effect of inflation on the value of assets and the use of interest-free loans on a large scale to transfer real wealth free of tax. It is imperative to tax such loans as the lack of interest charged could be regarded as a taxable capital transfer. It is also necessary to look at generation-skipping devices such as trusts. These should also be subjected to the tax.

A capital transfer tax has certain advantages over an inheritance tax, although the latter takes account of the ability to pay which the donee or heir acquires. On balance the former seems preferable at this stage.

Property tax
The possibility of introducing a national (fixed) property tax should be investigated. At the moment rates on property collected by local authorities vary from authority to authority. It also leaves the possibility that some local authorities, even after the introduction of a single tax base, could maintain rates lower than in other areas. This inequality would be further enlarged if local authorities were to be responsible for their own property valuations.

In an urban context investigation should be made into a property tax, imposed nationally (or regionally) and on indexed and regularly revalued fixed property, on which a local premium could be piggy-backed; such tax should be earmarked for grants to local authorities according to a set formula. It may also be desirable to make such a tax progressive, subject to the constraint that productive improvements (investments) should not be taxed as this would be taxing the source of growth. The tax will add to the progressivity of the tax system without a significant disincentive effect.

In a rural context, investigation should be made into a land tax, perhaps likened to a 'rural development tax', earmarked for development of small-scale farming and rural development. Such a tax could be levied on the value of agricultural land, and then be fully earmarked for agrarian reform. This would not only ensure that the required resources are made available, but would also mean that the proceeds would stay in the agricultural sector and help it to develop. Such an earmarked land tax would contribute to the perception of the tax system as fair.

TAX POLICY AND INVESTMENT
For our purposes tax policy may affect investment in two areas – domestic private investment and foreign investment. These will be discussed in turn.

Tax policy and domestic private investment

Tax policy may impact on domestic private investment in many direct and indirect ways. Space does not allow these to be discussed here. Instead I shall concentrate on some lessons to be drawn from recent international experience.

All industrial economies, many NICs and even some developing countries have in recent years introduced tax reforms which attempt to address various factors which might have an impact on investments. An important feature of most tax reforms of the 1980s was the reduction of rates on income taxes, both personal and corporate, thus aiming at increasing the investible surplus of private investors. This rests on the implicit assumption, of course, that the state will either invest that proportion of profits which is taxed less productively or will subject it to a higher propensity to consume.

In the case of a specific tax, it can be argued that there is a tendency for the economic cost of taxation to increase more than proportionately with the rate of taxation. The narrower the base, the higher the tax rate will have to be to generate a given amount of revenue. The higher, in turn, will be the economic cost associated with that rate. Theoretically, it can be argued that firms and households will shift resources from heavily taxed activities to lightly taxed ones. To the extent that this shift will result in a more inefficient allocation of resources, with possible harmful effects on the growth rate, it entails an economic (or efficiency) cost.

Tables 3.3 and 3.6 show that every OECD country has reduced the top or high rates since 1986. While these reforms may appear to have a positive effect on the disposable income of high-income earners available for saving or investment, they were often carried out under the constraint that they be revenue-neutral. In some cases this required offsetting the revenue loss (as a result of rate reductions) against the revenue gain from base-widening; in other cases the revenue loss from an overall reduction in the yield from one tax was offset by increasing the yield from another tax – for example, income tax losses were sometimes offset by the introduction of a VAT.

In many of the OECD countries the reduction of the top personal income-tax rates was partly offset by widening the base. In the case of personal income tax, it took on mostly two forms: either abolishing or limiting (usually by ceilings) tax reliefs for specific expenditures (e.g. home ownership and business expenses), or bringing in new forms of income into the tax base or widening the definition of such taxable income (e.g. fringe benefits and capital gains).

It seems as if the typical area for reduction or removal of tax expenditures (in the case of personal income tax) would be mortgage and other interest payments, welfare and fringe benefits, and social security contributions. Another recent technique to broaden the tax base is that of providing an alternative minimum tax (e.g. as a percentage of gross income – as in Canada and the United States) or a supplementary gross or nearer-to-gross income tax (Denmark and Norway). These taxes apply only to the highest-income groups, who are thereby prevented, through the use of tax reliefs such as interest deductibility, from reducing their liability below a basic minimum.

It is difficult, however, to conclude whether personal income-tax reforms have increased the availability of investible funds (although some countries have experienced an increase in household savings). They have certainly not reduced it. Moreover, the overall economic climate may remain the most important determining factor.

Turning to corporate income tax, we have already noted the extensive rate-flattening which occurred during the late 1980s (Table 3.6). It has also been introduced in many developing countries (OECD, 1990b). This has been partly offset by a broadening of the tax base through a reduction or elimination of incentives and concessions.

Table 3.6.   Changes in rate structure of corporate income tax of central government[a]

Country	Basic rate 1986	1990
Germany[b]	56	50
Greece	49	46
Italy[b]	36/10	36/10
Japan	43[c]	37.5[c]
Spain	35	35
Sweden[d]	52	30
Turkey	46	46
United Kingdom	35[c]	35[c]
United States[b]	15/18/30/40/46	15/25/34
Unweighted mean of all OECD	43	36
South Africa	50	50

Notes: [a]The table does not refer to the reduced rates for certain specified industries and qualified companies in a number of countries including Greece. [b]Countries with corporate taxes at subordinate levels of government. [c]There is a reduced rate of tax for small enterprises. [d]The rate for Sweden refers to 1991.
Source: Owens (1990).

Up to the mid-1980s, tax incentives were widely used to encourage investment. In some cases these incentives took the form of a general investment allowance or credit, and in others they were directed at specific assets, activities or regions.

Governments use explicit investment incentives in addition to those implicit in the tax treatment of depreciation, interest, and so forth. Special investment incentives include exemptions, tax allowances, tax credits, or special tax reliefs designed to assist particular groups or activities in specific industries or locations. These incentives serve either to reduce or to defer tax liability; the latter corresponds to an interest-free government loan over the deferment period. Tax incentives for special purposes, however, are often *ad hoc* and poorly integrated into the overall tax structure.

One effect of these measures was that investment in capital, particularly machinery and plant, was heavily subsidised. Many countries later came to take the view that these measures were not achieving the original objectives, but were merely distorting investment decisions. The experience in South Africa with investment incentives tends to correspond with these expectations. There has recently, therefore, been a move away from such incentives. Many developing countries, however, still retain extensive investment incentives, in spite of the uncertainty about their effectiveness.

In general, the effectiveness of a tax is inversely related to the number of goals it is meant to achieve. Tax incentives overload tax instruments with multiple objectives. They complicate compliance and prompt unproductive efforts to obtain their benefits. If the incentives are small, the economic gains are likely to be limited. If they are large, the erosion of the tax revenue base is likely to be significant.

The tax system is not the only, and by no means even the most important, factor in shaping the investment decisions of private investors. Many other considerations feature in the investment decisions of firms and individuals. The political, institutional, legal and macroeconomic environments and non-tax incentives all play a part in the decision to invest the surplus of a firm (or to borrow in order to invest). In short, the most important determining factor may well be the firm's expectations about the future.

Tax policy and direct foreign investment
International investment is highly mobile. In addition to government tax policies, there are many complex determinants of the flow of direct foreign investment. Non-tax economic considerations relating to the factors affecting the rate of return on capital investment undoubtedly play a major role. Non-economic factors, in particular the political and institutional environment in the host country, also weigh heavily in the decisions of the multinational firms on where to invest.

Tax incentives which were quite popular during the 1950s and 1960s have gradually lost their appeal, since the results were more modest than anticipated and since they tended to favour those with the highest ability to pay. Moreover, if the incentive mechanism is not believed to be sustainable, entrepreneurs could shy away from long-term commitments. It has been argued that, in any event, tax incentives tend to encourage short-term investment. A case can be made that the best environment for attracting foreign direct investment, given other prerequisites (non-tax factors), is not one of generous tax incentives but of relatively low tax rates for all business and a low government deficit, which would contribute to convincing prospective investors that the tax environment is indeed stable and durable.

In conclusion, it needs to be reiterated that the foreign investor is likely to take account of non-tax factors that have to be complementary to a favourable tax environment. These would include political stability; the existing institutional and regulatory framework, including protection of and restrictions on foreign investment; access to international as well as domestic credit; labour market provisions and practices; and macro-policies that include stabilising influences such as an overall policy environment that tends to reduce capital flight, currency substitution and the like.

CONCLUSION

We have explored a wide range of issues which need to be considered in developing an appropriate tax policy for a democratic South Africa. It now remains, in conclusion, to draw all of this together.

A viable and sustainable programme of redistribution is only possible if the expenditure side of the budget is used primarily to effect this, thus leaving to the tax side the task of raising as much revenue as possible, subject to the constraints of stability and growth. In designing an appropriate tax system it is necessary to consider the perceived fairness of each tax and the tax structure as a whole, in the context of the need to ensure efficiency.

South Africa is probably already approaching the maximum overall tax level which the economy can bear, given the present level of development and growth rate. Therefore total tax revenue as a proportion of GDP can only increase at a moderate annual rate, perhaps at about 0,5 per cent, and probably at a maximum of 1 per cent, of GDP per annum, provided the economy is growing.

This notion is supported by the fact that much of government expenditure which is not merely consumptive will only lead to increased productivity over a relatively long period of time, particularly in South Africa where 'social investment' has been so inadequate and wasteful in the past. Care must consequently be taken not to allow taxes to increase at a rate faster than that which the economy can bear.

A balanced tax system consisting of a whole range of direct and indirect taxes is better than a tax system which attempts maximum progressivity for its own sake. This also requires that top tax rates should not be too high and that we should not ignore the significant international trend towards a more balanced tax structure. This includes the broadening of the tax base by removing exemptions and deductions which often serve as avoidance loopholes.

The wealthy often receive income in the form of a capital gain. Equity demands that these accretions to the taxpayer's economic power also be taxed with a capital gains tax. This will also add to the perception of the tax system as fair.

There is a case to be made for the introduction of a minimum tax on businesses to compensate for the very low effective income-tax rate found in practice. One possible base for such a tax is value added in the business. A very low tax rate will raise considerable revenue because of the huge base. Being a minimum tax, it only provides a threshold below which income tax cannot fall. It thus falls away as income tax exceeds the threshold.

The case for a wealth tax is not clear and unambiguous. Until this has been studied more fully, the taxation of capital should be done through the comprehensive taxation of gifts and inheritances rather than through an annual wealth tax in the form of a capital transfer tax. A national property tax, imposed nationally (or regionally) and on an indexed and regularly revalued fixed property, on which a local premium could be piggy-backed, and earmarked for grants to local authorities according to a set formula, should be investigated. A case can be made for such a tax to be progressive.

It is suggested that in the context of rural property a land tax, or 'rural development tax', earmarked for the development of small-scale farming and rural development, should also be considered. Such a tax could be levied on the value of agricultural land, and then be fully earmarked for agrarian reform.

It is now widely agreed that tax incentives do not achieve the original objectives. In general, the effectiveness of a tax is inversely related to the number of goals it is meant to achieve. Tax incentives overload tax instruments with multiple objectives. The desirability of removing all incentives to investors warrants further investigation. This also applies in the case of foreign direct investment.

A case can be made that the best environment for attracting foreign direct investment, given other prerequisites, is not one of generous tax incentives but of relatively low tax rates for all business and a relatively low government deficit, which would contribute towards convincing prospective investors that the tax environment is indeed stable and durable. The foreign investor is likely to take account of non-tax factors that have to be complementary to a favourable tax environment. These would include political stability, the legal and institutional framework, and macroeconomic policies.

4

Deficit financing and redistribution in South Africa

BRIAN KAHN

Government budgets are often seen as a major means of stimulating economic growth and of effecting policies for redistribution. However, over the past two decades attempts by African and Latin American governments in particular to bring about growth and redistribution through large budget deficits (revenue shortages) have had disastrous economic consequences. This has resulted in hyperinflation, overvalued real exchange rates and capital flight. The economic adjustment to such events typically requires a real exchange rate depreciation, lowering of real wages and the cutting of budget deficits, policies which in the end harm those most who were the intended beneficiaries of such programmes.

In South Africa there is a need to reconcile the massive legitimate demands for government social expenditure whilst maintaining macroeconomic balance in order to prevent the country from following the Latin American scenario. As will be seen, the South African economy has not been characterised by excessive budget deficits. However, growing demands for increased social and welfare expenditure facing both the current government and to a greater extent a future government, are likely to start exerting pressure to increase the size and alter the composition of the deficit. This chapter is an attempt to highlight some of the implications of deficit financing and the constraints which face policymakers. Because decisions regarding the way in which government budget deficits are to be financed fall within the realm of monetary policy, the interrelationship between fiscal policy and monetary policy will be discussed. The conduct of both monetary and fiscal policy is in turn dependent on the nature of the exchange rate regime, and the relationship to exchange rate policy will also be analysed.

RECENT TRENDS IN SOUTH AFRICA'S BUDGET DEFICIT AND PUBLIC DEBT

In this section, trends in the budget deficit and public debt in South Africa will be analysed. It is not only the size of the budget deficit that is important but also the levels of government expenditure and taxes, as a given deficit

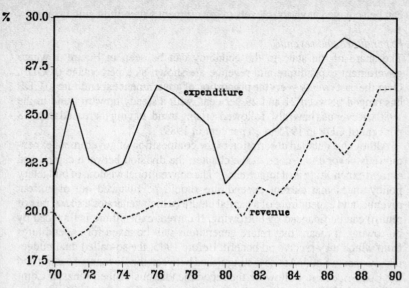

Fig. 1.   Government expenditure and revenue as a percentage of GDP

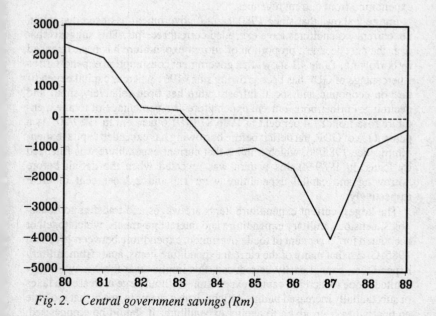

Fig. 2.   Central government savings (Rm)

can be achieved at various levels of government expenditure and taxation.

Expenditure and revenue

The share of the state in the economy can be seen in Figure 1 where government expenditure and revenue are shown as a percentage of GDP. Over the past twenty years the proportion of government expenditure to GDP has ranged between 21 and 29 per cent, with a steady upward trend in the 1980s. Revenues have also followed a rising trend, having increased from 18 per cent of GDP in 1971 to 26 per cent in 1989.

Although a detailed description of the composition of government expenditure is beyond the scope of the chapter, the division between capital and current expenditure is of importance.[1] The conventional wisdom of budgetary policy states that current expenditure should be financed out of current revenue, and expenditure of a capital nature (which generates a social rate of return) can be financed by borrowing. If current expenditure is financed by borrowing, it means that future generations will be taxed for expenditures from which they receive no benefit. Before 1975, the so-called dual budgetary system in South Africa distinguished between the Revenue Account and the Loan Account. Following the recommendations of the Franzsen Commission of 1970, a unitary budgetary system was adopted in 1976 whereby all government expenditure was funded out of the State Revenue Fund. This meant that there was no longer pressure on the authorities to finance current expenditure from current revenues.

Figure 2 shows that since 1980, central government has been dissaving, i.e. current expenditures have exceeded current receipts. This suggests that over the past decade a proportion of current expenditure has been financed by borrowing. Table 4.1 shows that government consumption expenditure as a percentage of GDP has been growing since 1961 whereas capital expenditure on economic and social infrastructure has been relatively small and declining. Furthermore, current expenditure as a percentage of total expenditure rose from 87,4 per cent in 1986/87 to 91,6 per cent in 1989/90. As a percentage of GDP, the deficit before borrowing has exceeded capital expenditure since 1985/86, which implies that current expenditure was financed by loans. In 1989/90 this pattern was reversed when the deficit before borrowing and capital expenditure were 1,5 and 2,2 per cent of GDP respectively.

The largest current expenditure items are wages and transfers to households, pensions, military expenditure and interest payments, which together accounted for 75 per cent of total government expenditure between 1980 and 1985. Given that many of the current expenditure items, apart from military expenditure, cannot easily be reduced, this implies that there may be only limited scope to increase capital expenditure without large increases in taxes or substantially increased budget deficits. It also seems to imply that too little emphasis has been given to capital expenditure. It should be emphasised, however, that the distinction between capital and current expenditure is not

clear-cut as all expenditures on human capital (e.g. education) are regarded
as current expenditure. What is required is a careful reclassification of
expenditures before any policy implications or conclusions can be drawn.

**Table 4.1   Government current and capital expenditure
(as percentage of GDP)**

CURRENT EXPENDITURE

	Consumption expenditure	*Interest payments*	*Other*	*Total*
1961–65	10,5	0,8	3,2	14,2
1966–70	11,3	1,2	3,3	15,8
1971–75	12,6	1,4	3,4	17,4
1976–80	14,3	2,4	3,9	20,5
1981–85	16,6	3,6	4,8	24,9

CAPITAL EXPENDITURE

	Economic infrastructure	*Social infrastructure*	*Total*
1961–65	2,7	0,9	3,3
1966–70	2,7	1,4	4,0
1971–75	2,7	1,7	4,4
1976–80	2,0	1,7	3,7
1981–85	1,5	1,3	2,8

Source: Le Roux and van der Walt (1987), p. 280

Trends in the deficit
In analysing trends in the budget deficit it is necessary to distinguish between
the primary deficit and the deficit before borrowing (or conventional deficit).
The latter is the difference between total fiscal expenditure and revenue,
where fiscal expenditure includes payments of interest on the public debt.
The primary deficit is the difference between total fiscal expenditure and
revenue, adjusted for interest and amortisation payments on the public debt.
It is often argued that this is the appropriate measure to analyse in terms of
the potential crowding-out effect on private investment.[2]

The ratio of the deficits to nominal GDP can be seen in Figure 3. Since the
late 1970s primary deficits have been small and at times have reflected a
surplus. This indicates that budgetary policy has in fact been conservative
throughout the 1980s. The difference between the primary deficit and the
conventional deficit reflects interest payments, and the increasing gap between the two measures reflects the higher interest rates that have been a
feature of the past decade.

Government debt
Although the stock of government debt has increased in nominal terms from

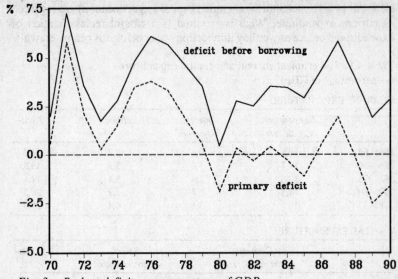

Fig. 3. Budget deficit as a percentage of GDP

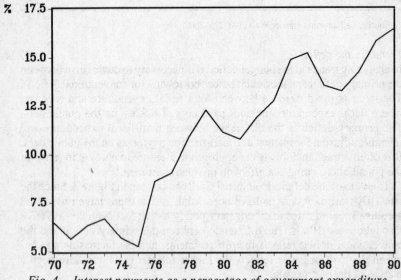

Fig. 4. Interest payments as a percentage of government expenditure

R4 764m in 1968/9 to R81 124m in 1989/90, the ratio of public debt to GDP has declined from 48,2 per cent of GDP to 34,8 per cent over the same period. Since 1983, the debt–GDP ratio has been constant at around 34 per cent. Government debt policy has not been excessive; since 1970, the only years which have seen the growth of government debt significantly exceeding that of the GDP, were 1976, 1977 and 1982.

However, as noted, what is important is the degree to which this debt is financing capital expenditure, which will then affect the future of GDP growth and therefore the future taxable capacity of the economy. In addition, the interest cost of the debt is of significance. During periods of rising interest rates, the ratio of interest payments on government debt to total government expenditure will increase and cause problems for the sustainability of the budget deficit.

Interest payments on government debt
As mentioned above, the difference between the primary deficit and the net deficit before borrowing is the level of interest payments paid on government debt. Figure 4 shows that the proportion of interest payments to total government expenditure (excluding loan redemptions) has increased substantially since 1975. In 1988/9, interest payments constituted 16 per cent of total government spending and this was exceeded only by the amounts budgeted for the defence and police, and education. The growing trend in interest payments is to a large extent the result of the Reserve Bank's monetary policies, which affect the levels of interest rates and the rate of inflation.

During inflationary periods, higher nominal interest rates compensate holders of debt for the declining real capital value of debt holdings. Rising interest rates imply that interest payments become a larger component of government expenditure. This means that a larger proportion of future tax revenues must be devoted to debt service and not to public services.

Trends in the financing of the deficit and public debt management
Public debt management is defined as 'the decisions, and implementation of these decisions, regarding changes, and the timing of such changes, in the size, the composition by type of security, the maturity structure, and the ownership of the public debt outstanding, more particularly and primarily the outstanding debt of the central government' (Meijer, 1986, p. 470). In South Africa, public debt management is the joint responsibility of the Department of Finance and the Reserve Bank. In financing the fiscal deficit, the maturity structure of debt issues is important as this will determine to an important degree the types of institutions that will be taking up the debt. This in turn could determine the macroeconomic impact of the deficit financing.

According to the conventional view, the impact of fiscal deficits on inflation will depend on the nature of the financing of the deficit – i.e. whether it is financed through borrowing or through money creation. Borrowing from the non-bank private sector is seen to be less inflationary as the deficits are financed by issuing non-money IOUs. In this case a debt issue would raise interest rates and therefore reduce private sector expenditure. If the debt is monetised through debt issues being taken up by the Central Bank, inflation could result. In this case the money creation will lead to a decline in interest rates and therefore increase overall expenditure.

The major reason why governments would choose to finance deficits by means of money creation relates to the nature of the domestic financial system. In the case of countries with undeveloped and thin capital markets, the government will be forced to sell debt to the Central Bank. As Cukierman has argued, 'in such countries, the ratio of government deficits to private savings is so large that any attempt to finance most or all of the deficit by tapping private capital markets leads to very strong pressures on real rates.... In such countries the pressures on the policy maker to monetise the deficit are much stronger than in the U.S. and some Western European countries' (Cukierman, 1987, p. 48). If the pressure on capital markets causes an increase in real interest rates above the real growth rate of the economy, then an increase in the deficit must involve in the future either a contraction of expenditure or monetisation by the Central Bank to maintain the debt at existing levels. Otherwise, the debt will keep expanding as the government has to increase borrowing in order to pay the increased interest commitments on debt previously incurred. It is clear then that the development of the domestic capital markets is important and that the ratio of government deficits to private savings should not increase sufficiently to cause excessive increase in real interest rates or the emergence of inflation- financed deficits.

In South Africa, the four major sectors which take up government debt issues are the foreign sector, the domestic monetary banking sector (including the Reserve Bank), the non-bank private sector (particularly the life assurance companies and the private pension funds) and the Public Investment Commissioners (PIC). Table 4.2 shows the ownership distribution of total government debt whilst Table 4.3 shows the institutions that have taken up new issues of debt in each fiscal year. From these tables it can be seen that the bulk of Treasury issues are directed to the domestic capital market (the non-banking private sector) or the Public Investment Commissioners. The latter body receives funds from the public sector for long-term investments and administers a range of funds on behalf of the public sector.[3] The PIC are required by law to invest all funds in fixed interest stock of the government or other public sector issues of stock. At least 75 per cent of the assets administered by the PIC have to be invested in RSA government stock. As can be seen from Tables 2 and 3, the PIC is the major holder of marketable government stock and annually finances a significant proportion of the Treasury's loan requirements.

In effect, the PIC are a captive market for a significant proportion of debt issues. In addition, as the Department of Finance has noted, 'the PIC are seldom in competition with private sector institutions. This is because the

PIC do not normally submit a competitive tender for government stock. In the annual budget the allocation of government stock to the PIC is determined on the basis of the PIC's own expected requirements, as well as those of the government' (Department of Finance, quoted in Falkena *et al.*, 1986, p. 113). They are, however, active in the secondary capital market and in this respect they compete with other capital market institutions.

Table 4.2 Ownership distribution of domestic marketable government debt (expressed as percentages)

	1979	1984	1985	1986	1987	1988	1989
Short-term[a]							
P.I.C.	10,9	7,0	2,1	1,6	2,3	6,3	7,3
Reserve Bank	0,8	–	2,9	0,6	–	0,8	2,9
C.P.D.	4,0	2,6	1,9	4,2	2,3	–	0,6
Banking sector[b]	79,0	59,1	46,9	67,9	61,9	73,7	62,8
Insurers[c]	1,0	26,0	32,8	18,7	21,5	15,1	16,1
Other	4,3	5,2	13,3	7,0	12,0	4,1	10,2
Long-term							
P.I.C.	58,8	44,1	49,2	52,4	56,1	55,7	52,0
Reserve Bank	0,9	1,3	1,8	1,4	0,7	1,7	0,9
Banking sector	8,7	5,9	4,6	2,6	1,7	1,7	0,9
Insurers	28,1	36,6	34,2	30,6	29,4	29,8	31,1
Other	3,4	12,1	10,2	12,9	11,9	11,0	15,0

Notes: [a]Outstanding maturity not exceeding 3 years. [b]Including discount houses, commercial banks, merchant banks, general banks and building societies. [c]Insurers and private pension funds.
Source: Derived from *Statistical/Economic Review*, various issues.

Table 4.3 Financing of the exchequer deficit (R bn)

80/1	83/4	84/5	85/6	86/7	87/8	88/9
Internal sources						
P.I.C.	0,9	1,3	2,1	2,9	5,6	3,7	6,6
Paymaster	0,2	–0,5	0,3	–0,4	–0,5	0,1	–0,9
Pvt non-bank	0,6	1,7	3,2	0,5	0,9	3,6	4,8
Banking sector[a]	0,2	0,9	–1,2	1,4	0,9	3,3	–
Exchequer[b]	–1,2	1,0	–0,3	0,2	–	–0,1	–1,3
Foreign sector	–0,1	0,2	0,3	–1,4	–0,1	–0,1	–0,1
Total	0,5	4,6	4,4	4,5	6,9	10,6	9,2

Notes: [a]Change in holdings of government securities. [b]Change in Exchequer balance (increase–, decrease +).
Source: *Statistical/Economic Review*, various issues.

The bulk of the remaining capital market issues are taken up by the private pension funds and long-term life assurers. Although in the past there were prescribed asset requirements in terms of which pension funds had to hold up to 53 per cent of their assets in government stock, these requirements were abolished in 1984. The 1984 regulations required insurance companies to hold 33 per cent of new cash flows into life assurance policies in the form of any money market or capital market instrument. In 1989, the Prudential Investment Guidelines reduced this to 15 per cent of the market value of assets. The result of this is that the captive market for government stock has effectively been limited to the PIC. This has meant that interest rates on long-term government stock have had to be more market-related than in the past and could account, in part, for the increased proportion of interest payments in government expenditure. The higher yields have also meant the insurance companies' holdings of government stock have not declined much.

From Table 4.3 it can also be seen that there has not been excessive reliance on the banking system to take up the new debt issues.[4] As can be seen in Table 4.2, Reserve Bank holdings of government securities make up a small proportion of total outstanding government debt. Although the banking sector holds a significant proportion of short-term debt, over 80 per cent of public debt issues have a maturity structure of more than three years.

In recent years, the foreign sector has declined in importance as a source of borrowing for deficit financing purposes because of the closure of international money and capital markets to South African borrowers following the 1985 debt crisis. South Africa's external borrowing has been determined over time by the willingness of international banks to extend credit to South Africa. Foreign debt as a proportion of total debt peaked at 11 per cent in 1976. Following the closure of the markets to South Africa after the Soweto revolt, the ratio declined to 3 per cent in 1980. During the early 1980s, South Africa had easier access to foreign credit – albeit at much shorter maturities. By 1985, foreign debt accounted for 12 per cent of total debt. However, after the closure of the foreign markets to South Africa in 1985, the percentage of foreign debt to total debt declined to 2,5 per cent in 1989.

Although the foreign sector has become an insignificant source of deficit financing, the implications of foreign borrowing should be considered in the light of the lifting of financial sanctions. The perceived advantage of external borrowing for budgetary reasons is that it takes the pressure off domestic money and capital markets and reduces the need for raising domestic taxes. In addition, foreign borrowing results in an increase in foreign exchange reserves. The apparent short-run attractiveness of external borrowing, however, hides the potential longer-term problems associated with persistent borrowing. The major problem is that of repayment of the interest and principal in the future. Unless budget deficits are used to finance growth-inducing expenditures that can raise future revenues, future taxes will have to be raised. This could involve an increase in the real burden of debt particularly in the face of a real domestic currency depreciation.

THE RELATIONSHIP BETWEEN FISCAL POLICY, MONETARY POLICY AND EXCHANGE RATE POLICY

Monetary policy and interest rates

In South Africa, financial policies exert their influence on redistribution through their impact on interest rates, the inflation rate and the exchange rate. Whether or not public debt issues do in fact affect interest rates and inflation depends to a large degree on the Reserve Bank's monetary (or interest rate) policy.

As Whittaker and Theunissen (1987) and Meijer (1986) have argued, the Reserve Bank's monetary policy is interest rate policy. Banks are required to hold certain minimum levels of cash reserves in the form of vault cash and as balances on their reserve accounts with the Reserve Bank. If the banks find themselves short of reserves, they are able to borrow from the Reserve Bank by rediscounting certain acceptable short-term assets at the discount window. The rate at which the Bank provides assistance to the banking system is the rediscount rate. The value of the banking system's indebtedness to the Bank is known as the money market shortage or accommodation. If banks need to offset a loss of reserves, they will 'borrow' from the Reserve Bank, thereby increasing the money market shortage. Banks will avoid holding excess cash balances because no interest is earned on them and because the Reserve Bank refinancing facilities are automatically and unconditionally available to them to make good any deficiency in cash balances. Thus if the banks find themselves with excess reserves, they will use these reserves to retire previous debt incurred at the discount window, i.e. the money market shortage declines.

By maintaining the money market shortage at some positive level (i.e. keeping the banks indebted to it) the Reserve Bank is able to determine short-term interest rates as accommodation is always available at a cost that the Bank chooses. The Reserve Bank maintains a positive money market shortage through open market operations (buying or selling bonds), changing the amount of treasury bills offered at its weekly tender, and by varying minimum cash balance requirements.

Because accommodation is extended automatically and unconditionally, money market rates for a given rediscountable instrument will approximate the Reserve Bank's rediscount rate. This is because if the market rate on, say, bankers' acceptances (BA's) is lower than the rediscount rate, then an institution holding BA's under rediscount will want to reduce its amount of BA's, as it would earn more on rediscounts purchased from the Reserve Bank than on BA's purchased in the market. Conversely if the market rate is higher than the rediscount rate, institutions will want to offer more paper for rediscounting. In this case, by trying to buy rediscountable paper that can be passed on to the Bank, the price of the instrument will be bid up in the market, thereby reducing the market interest rate until it equals the Bank's rediscount rate. It should be noted, however, that there are instances when the two rates can diverge significantly. This is particularly the case when the market expects the Reserve Bank to change its rediscount rates. Thus if the market expects the Reserve Bank to reduce the Bank rate in the near future, because the associated refinancing rates will also be lower, market rates will decline below the current rediscount rate. This divergence will be unsustainable if the Bank does not in fact reduce the rediscount rate.

It also follows that if the money market shortage is eliminated, the Reserve Bank would no longer be able to determine short-term interest rates. Because the banks will have retired all previous debt incurred, their excess reserves will have to be lent out. In order to induce the public to increase their borrowing, lower rates of interest will have to be charged.

Because long-term rates are an approximate average of expected future short-term rates, long-term rates will also be affected by a change in short-term rates. As Whittaker argues, 'in determining long-term rates, market participants are implicitly forming a view of the Reserve Bank's reaction to future expected values of the inflation rate, output, and other variables. If, for instance, inflation is expected to rise in the future, then the Bank may be expected to react by raising the bank rate, and this general expectation would be reflected by higher current long- term rates than short' (Whittaker, 1987, p. 14).

The implication of the above is that the Reserve Bank affects the economy through its influence on interest rates and not directly through controlling the money supply. Thus if the authorities reduce the bank rate, commercial bank rates will fall, resulting in increased demands for bank credit. This causes an increase in bank deposits and larger required reserves which are obtained through accommodation. In this case, lower interest rates cause the money supply to rise because of increased demands for bank credit, which are then accommodated. Thus the Reserve Bank's influence on the economy comes directly through its choice of interest rate, which in turn affects the general level of expenditure in the economy.

It should be noted that the interest rate objectives have at times been inconsistent and variable. In 1983–5 the main objective of the Reserve Bank was to combat inflation. This resulted in the prime overdraft rate rising to 25 per cent in 1984. Because of the impact of these high rates on unemployment, this policy was reversed and by 1986 rates had fallen to 12,5 per cent. Interest rates remained relatively low until the increase in domestic investment in late 1987 started putting pressure on the current account of the balance of payments in the face of debt repayments on the capital account. Interest rate policy then became determined by the balance of payments. Although during 1990 the large current account surpluses and the loosening of pressure on the capital account eased the balance of payments constraint, current interest rate policy is now directed at reducing the rate of inflation. One of the results of these changing policy objectives has been a highly variable real rate of interest, which has implications for the real cost of debt servicing.

Monetary policy and the fiscal deficit

If the Reserve Bank takes up a new issue of government debt under the current institutional arrangements in South Africa, when the funds are spent by the Treasury the banks will have excess reserves. These reserves will then be used to redeem paper on discount with the Bank. As this process continues, the money market shortage will disappear. At this point the Reserve Bank would lose control over short-term interest rates as the banks would attempt to increase lending to the public by offering loans at lower rates of interest. If the Bank wishes to maintain its control over interest rates it will need to maintain a positive money market shortage. One way it could achieve this is through open market operations, i.e. it could sell bonds to the public. Because the public will now be holding the government debt, the net result of government borrowing from the Reserve Bank will be the same as if the bonds were sold directly to the public in the first instance. Thus the need to maintain a positive money market shortage in order to maintain control over interest rates imposes an automatic constraint on financing deficits through money creation.

This does not imply, however, that there are no limits to deficit financing. Apart from the impact of the increased interest burden, there is a limit to the amount of debt that the capital market could absorb without putting upward pressure on real interest rates. If this were to occur, the authorities would be forced to allow the debt to be monetised, with possible inflationary consequences.

How public debt issues affect the general level of interest rates will therefore depend fundamentally on the Reserve Bank's discount policy and also on the market's expectation about the Reserve Bank's future interest rates. By selling government debt to the market, the Reserve Bank forces banks to seek accommodation which may or may not be at increased rates. In themselves, sales of long-term securities may have some upward effect on long-term rates. As Kock and Meijer note, 'sales of long-term securities may conceivably cause some (possibly temporary) upward pressure on long-term interest rates even if the money market rates continue to adhere closely to the level set by the Reserve Bank's rediscount rates. Such sales may also affect long-term interest rate expectations, perhaps because they are taken as evidence of the authorities' continuing anti-inflation monetary stance' (Kock and Meijer, 1987, p. 183).

It can be concluded, then, that there has been no necessary connection between fiscal deficits and interest rates. Because the interest rate is the instrument of monetary control it is determined by the Reserve Bank's policy objectives at the time. However, if the deficit had to become excessively large the capital markets would not be able to absorb all the new issues of debt without a substantial increase in interest rates. This would then increase the interest burden of the future budgets. If the authorities wish to avoid the impact on long-term interest rates, the debt could be monetised, i.e. the Reserve Bank would take up the debt issues and allow interest rates to fall, which could then conflict with anti-inflation objectives and balance of payments or exchange rate policy.

Fiscal policy, the balance of payments and the exchange rate

During the past decade, South Africa's exchange rate policy has been one of managed floating of the rand. Although the exchange rate is determined in the foreign exchange market, the Reserve Bank exerts its influence on the market through intervening by buying or selling foreign exchange. Both the real and nominal effective exchange rates have shown substantial movements, reflecting in part changes in the gold price and political shocks (see Kahn, 1991). Since 1988, it appears that the policy of the Reserve Bank has been to intervene in the market to maintain a constant real effective exchange rate, i.e. nominal exchange rate changes have been reflecting inflation rate differentials between South Africa and its major trading partners. Exchange rate policy has also been supplemented with restrictions on capital movements.

The relationship between the external sector and budget deficits must be considered in terms of the effects of the budget deficit on the balance of payments and the exchange rate. An increase in the budget deficit that increases expenditure will affect the balance of payments – for any given values of investment and savings, an increase in government expenditure relative to tax revenues will lead to a current account deficit. Put another way, during the past five years foreign debt repayment commitments have resulted in the need to run current account surpluses. This could have been brought about through increasing domestic savings, of both government and the private sector. An increase in the budget deficit which would reduce government savings would require an increase in private sector savings or a decline in investment. As domestic savings were declining over this period, it meant that the burden of adjustment was placed on reducing domestic investment. Interest rate policy then became directed towards preserving the current account surplus as higher interest rates reduce domestic investment. An excessive budget deficit that is monetised and reduces interest rates will therefore bring about a deterioration of the current account of the balance of payments and a loss of foreign exchange reserves. Alternatively, if the exchange rate is completely flexible, the rand will depreciate and impact negatively on the rate of inflation.

Thus monetary and fiscal policies are inextricably tied to exchange rate policy. An increased budget deficit which puts pressure on the current account could be offset by tight monetary policy (high interest rates) if the objective is to maintain a fixed exchange rate and avoid increased inflation. If fiscal policy is expansionary and interest rates are not allowed to increase, the impact will be on the level of foreign exchange reserves. Because exchange reserves are finite, eventually a change in policy will be forced on the authorities. Thus any given level of budget deficit will require an appropriate rate of interest to maintain a fixed exchange rate, which may conflict with other macroeconomic or redistributive objectives.

If the policy objective is to prevent a depreciation of the rand in the face of a large deficit, the rand will become increasingly overvalued. Exchange rate overvaluation results in a decline in a country's international competitiveness and therefore a reduction in exports. The combination of excessive budget deficits and exchange rate overvaluation has also been shown to be important determinants of capital flight in Latin America (see Lessard and Williamson, 1987). An important fiscal effect of capital flight is that it reduces the tax base. There is usually a strong presumption that capital that flees illegally is not likely to be reported domestically and the income earned on such assets is unlikely to be repatriated or declared. Dornbusch puts it strongly by arguing that 'public finance is wrecked by the pervasive habit of holding assets abroad and the associated tax fraud. ... [capital outflows] involve speculation against burdens that must be borne by society in the aggregate and most of the time are outright tax fraud' (Dornbusch, 1987, p. 145). Social infrastructure projects which might otherwise have been financed through tax revenues would have to be financed by borrowing to finance the increased fiscal deficit.

In the South African context, the interrelationship between fiscal policy and exchange rate policy has important consequences for the state's tax revenues from the gold-mining industry. In 1980 and 1981, income tax on gold mines accounted for approximately 25 per cent of inland revenue. Following the fall in the gold price, this proportion fell to an average of 8 per cent during 1982–7. By 1989, the contribution of mining taxation to inland revenue had fallen to 2,6 per cent. To a certain extent, gold-mining's contribution to tax revenues is determined not only by the dollar gold price but the rand gold price, which in turn is determined by the exchange rate. Until 1988, exchange rate policy appeared to be directed at maintaining the profitability of the mining industry by allowing for a depreciation of the rand during periods of a falling gold price. Since 1988, the Reserve Bank's policy has appeared to be directed at maintaining a constant real effective exchange rate. The result has been that the gold-mining industry is no longer protected against a falling dollar gold price by a depreciating rand. This has resulted in a significant decline in the profitability of the gold-mining industry. Declining gold-mining tax revenues, in both relative and absolute terms, have resulted in the need to increase other forms of taxation, including indirect taxes.

IMPLICATIONS AND CONCLUSION

Financial policies exert their influence on redistribution through their impact on interest rates, the inflation rate and the exchange rate. As we have seen, the Reserve Bank has direct control over the interest rate, which it can use as an instrument to achieve a particular objective. The interest rate cannot be used to achieve two conflicting objectives simultaneously. Thus, for example, the authorities would be unable to stimulate output (low interest rates) and control inflation (high interest rates) at the same time. As explained, low interest rates in the face of an increased fiscal deficit are likely to cause the deficit to be monetised and result in increased inflation.

Governments often prefer to have low interest rates as this reduces the cost of servicing the government debt. In addition, low interest rates stimulate employment and are politically popular particularly because of their effect on home mortgage rates. Interest rates that are 'too low', however, create their own problems. Firstly, they result in the stunting of the growth of domestic capital markets because of the disincentive to save. As we have seen, the development of long-term capital markets is essential as a source of mobilising domestic savings to finance government expenditure in a less inflationary way. The lack of such a market means that the authorities have no option but to rely on inflationary means of financing the deficit. South Africa at present has a relatively well-developed financial system and excessive reliance on inflationary deficit financing has not been a feature of the system. There is, however, a limit to the amount of issues the market can absorb without putting increased pressure on the real rate of interest.

Secondly, excessively low interest rates will put pressure on the balance of payments or the exchange rate or both. If the exchange rate is fixed, we will eventually run out of reserves. If the exchange rate is flexible, the domestic currency will depreciate, resulting in increased inflation. Related to this is the fact that if the exchange rate is fixed or managed, the resulting overvaluation of the exchange rate will inevitably lead to capital flight. Thus more savings will be lost to the country and the beneficiaries will be the wealth-holders who hold their assets abroad.

The above does not imply that there is no scope for increased mobilisation of resources for redistributive purposes or for reducing the burden of interest payments on government debt. One way that this could be achieved is through the reintroduction of a system of prescribed asset requirements, whereby capital market institutions would be required to hold a specified proportion of their assets in the form of government stock at low rates of interest. One of the effects of this would be to reduce the rate of return to policy-holders but could be justified as a means (implicit tax) of achieving some form of redistribution tax. However, the other impact would be to increase interest rates on private sector bond issues, which could impact negatively on private sector investment. Therefore an excessive deficit financed in this way could result in a significant decline (or crowding out) of private sector investment.

The literature on fiscal deficits tells us very little about the optimal level of debt. At best we can be mindful of the macroeconomic implications of different levels of debt. It must also be borne in mind that any debt incurred today will have to be repaid in the future. In other words, governments, like households, face an intertemporal budget constraint. There may be a strong case, for example, for increasing government debt during the period of transition towards democracy which could help ease the process of transition.

However, any increased transitional deficit will have to be balanced by a primary surplus in the future if an unsustainable deficit is to be avoided in the future.

A final implication of the above is that deficit financing should be used as productively as possible. That is, emphasis must be given to (appropriately defined) capital expenditure which generates a social return in the future. If deficit financing is undertaken to finance current consumption, it means that resources that could otherwise have been used for investment will now be used for consumption with no benefit for the future. To this end, care should be taken not to see the bureaucracy as a means of employment creation for this merely increases the level of current expenditure on unproductive activities.

5

Redirecting government expenditure

SERVAAS VAN DER BERG

The budget is still one of the major forms of economic discrimination in South Africa today. It is also the most effective instrument available for redistribution. Thus the expenditure side of the budget will have to bear a large part of the burden for ensuring a smooth transition towards sustainable democracy, for the stability of the political transition towards democracy will be determined by the ability of the new social and economic system to meet aspirations, especially those of the urban workforce. This chapter is a provisional attempt at addressing this issue. It does this by focusing on the broad parameters within which a redirection of government expenditure can take place to address social need and to move away from a political and economic system based on institutionalised inequality.

It is useful to start by considering these questions: What can we learn from public expenditures in other countries during the political development process? How much would it cost to eliminate 'fiscal apartheid'? What are the priorities in redirecting such expenditure? What is the scope for redirecting expenditures away from wasteful ideological and military purposes? Finally, what conclusions can be drawn from the above that will be useful for the transitional budgets away from apartheid?

International experience in public expenditure
The tendency for government expenditure to rise relative to the overall national product was first noted in the nineteenth century by the German economist Adolf Wagner. Though there is international debate on whether Wagner's 'law' actually holds for the reasons put forward by Wagner and whether it necessarily always applies (see e.g. Kohl, 1985; Leineweber, 1988; Recktenwald, 1981), there appears to be widespread acceptance that the 'law' does generally describe what occurs in the rise of countries from traditional societies to modern industrial states.

Of more particular interest to this chapter is the *composition* of public expenditure. International cross-section data give some pointers to likely trends in the development process (Zimmermann, 1981, p. 119; World Bank,

1988, p. 106):

— At low levels of development, the share of public investment expenditure in the budget is relatively high, especially for infrastructure (e.g. road building). Education and health expenditures also tend to rise from a low base in low-income countries, mainly to cater for lower levels of provision of these services (primary education, primary health care). Expenditure on export and other incentives to favour domestic industry is also often significant (as is tariff protection, though it is not reflected in public expenditure).

— In middle-income countries (such as South Africa), the demand for educational and health expenditure tends to rise, as does research and development expenditure, while the creation of a social security system typically starts receiving more attention, though it usually remains relatively small.

— At higher levels of economic development, the share of transfers (social security) as well as of public services tends to grow, whilst public investment shows a relative decline. According to Leineweber (1988, p. 292), this pattern indicates that the state increasingly tends to satisfy individual needs *directly* rather than indirectly.

But industrialisation is not the only factor. The political framework is also crucial. According to Kohl (1985, p. 167), in nineteenth century Europe extension of the franchise under constitutional monarchy led to an increase in the social and educational expenditure ratio (as a percentage of national product), as well as in spending on economic services, transport and infrastructure. This rise in social spending was partly financed from increased taxation and partly through reduced defence spending.

This appears to be similar to the likely effect of the extension of the franchise in South Africa today. (Even the very limited extension of the franchise under the tricameral parliament produced such an effect.) Whereas provision of social services was initially the driving force behind the increase in government expenditure in Western European countries and specifically in Germany, greater social transfer payments played the dominant role from the time of Bismarck's social reforms in the 1880s (Leineweber, 1988, p. 282). The substantial increases in government spending associated with mass democracy (as in industrial countries after World War Two) as compared to constitutional monarchies with an extended franchise (Kohl, 1985, p. 167) are not attainable in South Africa today. Such massive increases in social expenditure (mainly transfers in the forms of social insurance) are only affordable in much more affluent societies where the majority of the labour force is involved in the modern sectors of the economy. Terreblanche (1989) argues that the shift from nineteenth-century *laissez-faire* capitalism to twentieth-century democratic capitalism was mainly responsible for the increase in public expenditure in Europe, and that the dilemma in South Africa lies in reconciling democracy with a more limited tax capacity than was the case in European countries.

From this brief analysis, one would expect political change in a middle-income country such as South Africa to produce budgetary shifts towards greater provision of social services. However, a large-scale increase in social transfers associated with social insurance and the welfare state still appears premature in the light of the large-scale unemployment and underemployment of labour, the lack of an institutional basis for such transfers and, most important, resource constraints.

However, South Africa already has relatively high levels of expenditure on health and education, even though the major part of the population do not share equitably in these expenditures. Although rising social expenditure may seem desirable in terms of the needs of the disadvantaged sectors of our society, the scope for such shifts is constrained. For instance, South African educational expenditure in 1986 was already 5,6 per cent of gross domestic product (GDP), whilst the 'average' for middle-income countries was 2,9 per cent, and the highest value in such countries was 6,4 per cent in oil-rich Oman (World Bank, 1988). It thus appears as if greater educational expenditure for blacks would have to be financed mainly by reducing educational expenditure for whites.

Discrimination in social expenditure
Discrimination in social expenditure reflects the fact that the needs of whites have received far more attention than warranted, while those of blacks have received too little.

As can be seen from Table 5.1, parity within the constraints of the existing social budget in 1986 would have implied a two-thirds reduction in white benefits from government social expenditure on primary and secondary education, health and social pensions, to a point well below the level of benefits received by coloureds.[1] An increase in social expenditure on blacks as well as a great reduction in expenditure on whites was therefore required.

On the other hand, Table 5.1 shows that parity *at prevailing white levels of expenditure* in the allocation of government social expenditure on these items would have required an almost fivefold increase in social expenditure benefiting blacks, from R5,4 billion to R25,5 billion in 1986/7. This confirms that eliminating discrimination in public social expenditure patterns, without reducing resources devoted to whites, is a policy of vast immediate redistributive consequence, tantamount in its impact on the racial allocation of resources to a R27,5 billion increase in total black incomes in 1986 – and this does not even consider the impact on future black incomes through improving human capital. Regrettably, expenditure of this magnitude under present circumstances is simply unaffordable.

Reallocating *existing* social expenditures to achieve social spending parity is also a fundamental redistributive measure. It would have required reducing state resources allocated to whites by almost R3 billion in 1986/7, with an equivalent increase in financial resources devoted to blacks. Even if whites retained the same level of services by paying more for these services, the redistributive impact would have been similar, for that would have been

Table 5.1. Government social spending, 1986/7: actual and parity requirements[a]

	White	Coloured	Indian	African	Total
Total social spending (in billions of rand):					
Actual spending	4,3	1,7	0,5	5,4	11,9
Parity spending:					
at white levels[b]	4,3	3,5	0,9	25,5	34,2
within constraints[c]	1,5	1,2	0,3	8,9	11,9
Population (million)	4,9	3,0	0,9	25,2	33,0
Per capita social spending (rand):					
Actual spending	879	564	547	214	361
Parity spending:[d]					
at white levels	879	1 162	985	1 013	1 036
within constraints	307	398	328	353	361

Notes: [a] Social spending in this table includes only primary and secondary education, health, and social pensions. [b] I.e. raising everyone to the expenditure levels on whites. [c] I.e. equalising expenditures across races and holding down expenditures to current social spending levels. [d] The differences in per capita spending requirements for parity to be reached arise partly from the differential age structure that determines the clientele for social pensions and education, and partly from income differences causing fewer whites to require social pensions.

Source: Social spending figures based on data from *Race Relations Survey 1988* (cf. Van der Berg, 1989); population data based on Simkins (1990).

equivalent to a tax of similar magnitude.

In South Africa the budgetary shortfall in meeting social needs common to developing countries has been exacerbated by apartheid policies, which allowed white standards to be raised to unrealistic levels for a middle-income country, thereby raising expectations of all groups. The present dilemma is how to move towards parity. Four alternatives suggest themselves: (i) devoting a greater share of public spending to social spending; (ii) reducing spending on whites; (iii) dampening expectations of all South Africans to levels commensurate with the country's resources as a developing country rather than with present white benefits; and (iv) reconsidering methods of providing services to ensure that the most cost-effective delivery methods are used.

As will be shown, there is *some* scope for the first of the four options mentioned above of further increasing social spending at the expense of other public spending programmes, but there is less scope for this than is often thought. South African social expenditure ratios are not greatly out of line with other countries at comparable levels of economic development (Table 5.2). There is obviously a need for savings (as in the fourth option above) through restructuring the social service system itself, reducing duplication and increasing capacity utilisation. But the bulk of social expenditure cannot be avoided: social pensions, teacher salaries, medical personnel and equipment, etc. The real challenge is thus to adjust expectations of whites (and of other groups) downwards to a level commensurate with South Africa's resources as a developing country and to restructure social expenditure accordingly.

Table 5.2. Percentage of national product devoted to defence, education and health, 1986

Country	Proportion of national product devoted to:		
	Defence	Education	Health
Lower middle-income developing countries:			
Average	3,74	3,61	1,00
Highest	12,28	8,74	5,65
	(Jordan)	(Botswana)	(Costa Rica)
Upper middle-income developing countries			
Average	2,92	2,89	1,44
Highest	26,48	6,38	5,14
	(Oman)	(Oman)	(Panama)
South Africa	3,9[a]	5,6[a]	3,0[a]

Notes: [a] Expressed as proportion of GDP at market prices (R145,9 billion in 1986).
Sources: World Bank (1988); Calitz 1989, Table 2, p. 16.

Once political apartheid is abolished, major changes are required to abolish fiscal apartheid, but this would have to take place within the constraints of limited additional resources for social spending. It is disturbing, yet perhaps symptomatic of our politics, that politicians on both sides of the present racial divide conspicuously avoid publicly admitting that the effect of democratisation and the resultant need for horizontal fiscal justice (a more appropriate norm than parity in that it allows for the greater needs of the poor) would have to be a drastic reduction in social expenditures benefiting whites.

The results of a previous attempt (Van der Berg, 1989) at providing rough figures of the effect on social expenditure in four important and costly fields – education, social pensions, health, and housing – if spending across races were to be equalised at current white levels, and housing needs addressed, are summarised in Table 5.3. Social spending in these four fields would have had to increase from just under 10 per cent to between 25 and 31 per cent of GDP, or from less than R14 billion to more than R44 billion in 1986. This is clearly not attainable, even if it were possible to sharply reduce other public expenditure to far below the 17,9 per cent prevailing in 1986. Note that education is by far the most expensive item of the four, especially once parity is introduced at white levels. This is a consequence not only of the great educational needs, but also of the greater discrimination in education than in other fields, and the very expensive nature of present white education.

Table 5.3.   Costs of parity in social expenditure, and costs of meeting housing needs, in 1986 rand and as percentage of GDP at market prices

	Present expenditure		Conservative estimate[a]		Liberal estimate[a]	
	Rm	% of GDP	Rm	% of GDP	Rm	% of GDP
Education[b]	6,8	4,8	24,0	16,6	27,7	19,2
Social pensions[b]	1,9	1,3	3,7	2,6	5,2	3,6
Health[b]	4,0	2,8	6,0	4,2	8,0	5,6
Housing[c]	1,0	0,7	1,7	1,2	3,5	2,4
Total[d]	13,7	9,5	35,4	24,5	44,4	30,8
Other govt. expenditure		17,9		17,9[e]		17,9[e]
Total govt. expenditure		27,4		42,4[e]		48,7[e]

Notes: [a] Conservative and liberal: based on various assumptions regarding coverage, current levels of spending on whites, and different levels of housing provision. See Van der Berg (1989) for details. [b] Parity at current white levels, under various assumptions. [c] Upgrading, but not identical to parity *at white levels*, owing to the complexity of the assumptions required. See van der Berg (1989) for details. [d] The proportions of GDP do not always add up, because of rounding. [e] Assuming that other (non-social) government expenditure remains unchanged at 17,9 per cent of 1986 GDP at market prices, valued at R145,9 billion. (In Van der Berg (1989) these proportions were inadvertently shown relative to GDP *at factor cost*.)
Source: Van der Berg (1989).

The scope for redirecting public expenditure to meet needs.

In the past three decades, pressures for increased social spending were constrained by the black population's lack of access to political power. Yet social expenditures did rise, initially as a response to increased demands of white voters, but later increasingly in response to popular political pressure from other groups.

Government finance has since the late 1980s started showing all the strains of a fiscal crisis:
– rapidly rising tax ratios in a stagnant economy (much of it through fiscal drag) that led to a tax revolt amongst the middle classes and the breakdown of tax morality;
– a shift of resources away from capital expenditure to current expenditure;
– an increasing inability to fund operating, maintenance and other recurrent expenditure required to extend the life and utility of capital expenditure, 'because other spending demands ... exert stronger pressure on decision makers or lead to more visible disruption if not met' (World Bank, 1988, p. 115);
– an inability to contain actual expenditure within the bounds of the budget;
– retrenchment of subsidies to farmers and commuters as well as on basic foods; and
– a lack of legitimation of the political system which has resulted in attempts

at buying support, notably through increased educational expenditure and through public-sector wage increases aimed at retaining the support of the bureaucracy.

The evidence thus indicates that most of the fat has already been cut from the budget, and as its overall size is already large, there is little scope for increased funding by raising taxes or by increasing the deficit. This means a future government will inherit a budget that will leave it relatively little room for manoeuvre.

Savings from the abolition of apartheid

What, then, is the scope for increasing social expenditures? Table 5.2 showed that South African spending ratios were not that much different from those in other countries. It is also necessary, however, to consider the debate about the 'post-apartheid dividend'.

For years, opponents of apartheid have been arguing that apartheid is wasteful in its use of financial and human resources. Guesstimates of the cost of apartheid abound with questionable assumptions and arrive at greatly varying answers. The cost of apartheid has undoubtedly been greatest in its influence on the allocation and development of human resources. Its abolition can, for this reason, contribute to a substantial growth impetus through freeing resources and talents.

Yet it is far less certain that the abolition of apartheid will provide a great many *fiscal* resources for a new government. Admittedly, duplication of services and fragmentation of responsibilities under apartheid have created administrative nightmares and expanded the number of politicians and high-ranking officials considerably, many of them in the homelands. Yet the full homeland administration wage bill in 1985 did not much exceed one and a half billion rand, while the wage bill in Own Affairs departments reached about R2,1 billion (expressed in 1985 rand) in 1987.[2] When the full wage bill of the homelands and Own Affairs departments is thus added together, it amounted to less than R4 billion or about 3 per cent of GDP in 1985 – and most of this expenditure went on teachers, nurses and doctors. Thus it would be surprising if the cost of administering apartheid ever even approached 2 per cent of GDP; 1 per cent of GDP appears closer to the mark.

Administrative duplication is, however, not the only form ideological expenditure has taken. Decentralisation incentives to industrialists settling in or near the homelands have been rising. Almost a billion rand (R826 million in 1989) has been spent annually on such subsidies. This is a clear case of spending that could be slashed by immediately terminating the incentives for all new applicants and giving notice to existing entrepreneurs that these incentives are to be phased out. Such a step needs to be taken as a matter of urgency, for decentralisation incentives run for a number of years, and newly decentralising industries would thus still, have a claim on the fiscus for some years to come. A minimum of two years' notice is required for eliminating these incentives, but because of the abrupt effect on communities in some areas, a slower phasing-out of some incentives may be advisable.

The other remaining forms of ideological expenditure are relatively minor in their expenditure implications. Examples include the Group Areas Board and the Free Settlement Areas Board, each of which was allocated about half a million rand in 1990/91.

Another form of expenditure partly linked to the maintenance of apartheid is security and defence expenditure. Police expenditure in South Africa is relatively low; apartheid has reduced the efficiency of the relatively small police force in terms of its chief purpose, viz crime prevention. So there is no scope for decreasing police expenditure – quite the contrary. Thus, one more question remains: can defence spending be reduced, or, is there a peace dividend?

Is there a peace dividend?
Long-term structural shifts in defence spending can be appreciated from Table 5.4.

Table 5.4.   Defence spending as a percentage of GDP, 1912 to 1990

Year	Percentage	Year	Percentage
1912	0,8	1950	0,8
1920	0,4	1960	0,9
1930	0,3	1970	2,0
1940	3,0	1980	4,0
1943	7,5	1990	4,0

Source: Department of Finance, various years. *Estimate of the Expenditure to be Defrayed from the State Revenue Account During the Financial Year Ending 31 March.* Pretoria: Government Printer.

The initial displacement effect early in the 1970s (already noted by Seeber and Döckel in 1978) was caused by the Angolan war, defence spending rising from about 2,2 per cent of GDP in 1972 to a plateau above 4 per cent. The continued high level of defence expenditure can be explained by the decision to hang on to Namibia at virtually any cost and the triumph of 'total onslaught' thinking in government circles. Thus Browne refers to the success of the fiscus in financing *inter alia* 'a massive defence and rearmament effort' (Browne, 1983, p. 169).

If defence spending had not risen above its 1972 level of 2,2 per cent of GDP (a level which appears to be realistic for a peaceable regional power), the savings in the period 1973 to 1990 would have amounted to about R75 billion in 1990 rand. The opportunity cost of the Angolan war and the 'total strategy' against the 'total onslaught' was thus very great: this amount would have been adequate to build 1,9 million fully serviced houses, far in excess of the housing backlog of about 1,2 million units (according to Urban Foundation estimates).

Though these funds are irretrievably lost, the calculations give an indication of the gains to be made by reducing defence spending to more realistic levels, and doing so rapidly. This had already begun in 1989, when the defence spending ratio dropped half a percentage point. Further decreases are imperative.

Possible other cutbacks in expenditure

Based on the experience of the immediate past, it would appear as if the government is basing its hope for reducing other expenditures on further cutbacks in defence and on consumer subsidies (foodstuffs and commuting costs), decentralisation incentives, export subsidies, and university spending. Of these, only consumer subsidies are geared towards the needs of the poor.

There is a strong case to be made out for cutting the most expensive form of subsidisation, viz of suburban bus and train commuters. In 1990/1 the total cost of subsidies was about R1,5 billion for train commuting (much of it cross-subsidisation rather than direct subsidies) and R626 million for bus commuting.[3] Given their very large claim on resources, the relatively small number of beneficiaries, and the fact that there are other equally or more deserving claims on the budget, it is understandable that the government has long been trying to reduce the level of these subsidies. However, as these subsidies are large, phasing them out would severely affect the living levels of the affected commuters. The Department of Transport has estimated that these subsidies amount to about R2 500 per train passenger and R1 000 per bus passenger annually. In the case of train passengers, though, much of the subsidy consists of cross-subsidisation of services. The monthly income of subsidised passengers is R605 for train and R542 for bus passengers, which means that the subsidies paid to passengers are equivalent to a non-taxable addition of 34 per cent and 15 per cent respectively to their incomes.

Although the other items of expenditure mentioned above that the government is considering curtailing are all to a lesser or greater extent deserving of support, cutbacks may be appropriate if the needs of the poor are to be the priority.

In an 'alternative budget' in 1990, the Democratic Party attempted to show that there is considerable scope for improvement to the budget. While one would not quarrel with that contention, their suggested budget was far too optimistic. It was based on rapid economic growth (4,2 per cent averaged over five years), a reduction in non-social expenditure (no real growth in most such expenditures was allowed), additional cuts in defence expenditure (R3,4 billion), a reduction in state debt cost (R1,9 billion),[4] and savings of 'at least' R2 billion by reducing 'wasteful expenditure on apartheid/own affairs, quadruplication and ideologically based schemes such as industrial decentralisation'. It is small wonder that they arrived at a remarkably positive scenario in which additional revenue of R22,4 billion would become available for addressing social needs by the year 1995/6 (Democratic Party, 1990). Such an unrealistically positive scenario is downright dangerous if it contributes to postponing the very real critical choices that have to be made.

Other considerations in redirecting government expenditure
Redirecting government expenditure requires careful consideration of fiscal constraints. Other constraints also play a role, though, and the process necessarily needs careful planning. Aside from the fiscal resource constraints, some of the other considerations, such as the nature of the budgetary process, require more attention under a few broad headings:

(1) *Absorptive capacity in programme implementation limits the scope for redirecting expenditure in the short term.* A financial shift of resources towards social expenditure need not always imply an equal real shift of resources. For instance, increasing educational expenditure may run up against capacity constraints in the availability of teachers, textbooks and physical facilities, not to mention administration; increasing housing expenditure may similarly run up against bottlenecks in the provision of cement, bricks, and land. In such a case, the increased demand would just drive up the price and therefore the cost, and would in this way frustrate the whole aim of the budgetary shift.

(2) *Redirecting resources may have unintended consequences that affect a great many people.* It is important to consider possible side-effects of expenditure cutbacks, and keep in mind that effects go farther than the department directly concerned and may even change the livelihood of whole communities in particular localities. For instance, the sharp decrease in defence expenditure in 1990 caused military bases to close down. The reduction in arms purchases caused many Armscor plants to reduce their production or even close down, which had a major effect on employment and caused a sudden over-supply of certain categories of engineers. Similar results may flow from sharp cutbacks in allocations of funds to industrial decentralisation or aspects of the homeland administrations. It is preferable that the intention to cut back certain programmes should be made clear and that it should be put into practice over a few years, so that adjustment can be more gradual. The difficulty in expenditure cutbacks is exacerbated by the fact that well over half of government expenditure consists of personnel expenditure. Cutbacks in one programme do not necessarily imply that all resources can be smoothly transferred to other programmes.

(3) *Budgeting is an incremental process.* As budgeting is an incremental process, it is imperative that shifts of resources should be relatively gradual, though the needs may be great. Administrative structures are slow to be created, and once created cannot be abolished overnight without great trauma. Equally, demands met in one year create demands for future years. For instance, a large increase in pensions may seem advisable until other structures are in place to deliver services to the poor. But once granted, pension increases are difficult to cut back. A similar argument applies to increases in public-sector wage levels, which create costs that cannot be easily reduced in subsequent budgets. The previous mistake with white

education and white public-sector workers should not be repeated, for demands once met create future expectations that are very difficult to dampen.

(4) *In budgeting, one should guard against excessive optimism regarding future economic performance.* A former Secretary of Finance is of the opinion that the greatest mistakes in fiscal policy in South Africa in the past half a century were 'due to over-optimistic expectations of the progress of the economy' (Browne, 1983, p. 169). Over-optimism can lead to unrealistic planning and thereby to waste if resources are discovered to remain more scarce than expected.

(5) *The budget needs to be part of a longer-term economic strategy and needs to follow preset plans.* For the above and other reasons, some measure of indicative planning is required. The government should have a clear idea of where it is going, should make clear its intentions (as far as possible in quantitative terms), and should start getting the structures in place to carry out these intentions. Realistic targets in terms of shifts of resources and provision of services are useful both for the government's own planning and for the private sector and communities concerned, who can then base their expectations on them.

In the field of social services, it may be useful to work in terms of a transitional socio-economic plan, which may take five to ten years to implement fully. A ten-year plan for education, with a proper calculation of the resource costs and therefore the financial costs, would be very useful, in that it would allow educational administrators to put in place the required structures and to train the necessary teachers. At the same time, it would instil some realism in the community as to the time-span required to implement a policy of equal education. In health services, the planning framework may be shorter, perhaps five years. In the case of social pensions, on the other hand, parity need take only a year or two, as the administrative framework is already in place and the process is constrained only by financial resource allocations.

For this purpose, the present Economic Advisory Council is not appropriate; it is more of a business council than an economic council, and its brief should be expanded beyond the purely economic and beyond its present short-term bias to investigating socio-economic issues that are at the heart of the development debate in South Africa. A *Socio-Economic* Advisory or Planning Council seems more appropriate, and this should be reflected in its composition.

CONCLUSION

The foregoing analysis has shown that redirecting government expenditure is severely constrained by the scarcity of fiscal resources. Nevertheless, there is some scope for redirecting fiscal resources between programmes, mainly by reducing defence and ideological expenditures. Beyond that, greater social justice would especially have to be sought through a very substantial reduction in the public financial resources devoted to white education.

Budgeting remains an incremental process, thus change would have to reflect this. A clear determination of needs and priorities – i.e. a social welfare function – is required to take the debate about the budget much further, for the determination of priorities is the essence of the budgetary process. The extent of the fiscal resource constraints has become clearer; what is less clear and needs far more research and debate, is the choice of *priorities* in a post-apartheid economy. It is not enough to choose more butter and fewer guns – we should also decide how the butter is to be allocated, and how thinly it should be spread so that all can have some. In various areas of social need, we have been presented with some idea of the *expectations*, but that is not enough. We cannot have more university education and more food aid, and all the other doubtless desirable social services in unbounded quantities. In the end, further political debate on these issues is essential, but it needs to take place with full recognition of the resource constraints and of the opportunity costs. Only then will we be in a position to present an alternative budget that reflects the social welfare function of a democratic society.

6

Making welfare spending work

NICOLI NATTRASS & ANDRÉ ROUX

State spending is one of the more important mechanisms for effecting redistribution and alleviating poverty. By channelling resources through the budget from rich productive sectors of the economy to poverty-stricken regions and individuals, state institutions are able to have a significant impact on the employment opportunities and quality of life of the poor. This characteristic of the state, together with the influence it is able to exert on the economy by means of macroeconomic policies, makes government policy decisions a central focus in the struggle to create jobs, eliminate poverty and reduce inequality.

The close relationship between broader economic policies and welfare-specific programmes cannot be over-emphasised. In a recent survey of poverty, the World Bank makes the following observation: 'Rapid and politically sustainable progress on poverty has been achieved by pursuing a strategy that has two equally important elements. The first element is to promote the productive use of the poor's most abundant asset – labor.... The second is to provide basic social services to the poor. Primary health care, family planning, nutrition and primary education are especially important. The two elements are mutually reinforcing; one without the other is not sufficient' (1990, p. 3).

This chapter focuses predominantly on the second of these elements, viz extending the welfare net to poor people. We are particularly concerned about the very poor, i.e. the bottom 20–40 per cent of the income distribution. The policies proposed are therefore geared towards providing an acceptable 'bottom line' of welfare spending to the greatest number. The first section refers to the macroeconomic dimension while the second examines key microeconomic issues relevant to welfare strategies. The final sections deal with specific policies relating to health, nutrition and employment. Straightforward welfare transfers[1] are not discussed. Other major components of broadly defined welfare policy which are ignored are education and housing. Both of these require separate treatment.

MACROECONOMIC ISSUES
A growth strategy which takes full cognisance of balance of payments constraints and structural rigidities will generate a far more favourable context for the successful implementation of welfare-oriented policies than, for example, one which falls victim to stagflation – a malady which has beset many a country attempting to redistribute too much too quickly (Moll, 1988; World Bank, 1990, pp. 10–12). There are numerous examples where the temptation to print money in order to finance significantly increased levels of government spending has not only eroded real wages and had a particularly severe impact on the poor (Cornia and Stewart, 1990, p. 3), but has also provoked capital flight, reduced investment, shrunk the tax base by driving many economic activities into the informal and illegal sectors, led to misallocations of foreign exchange, and even to right-wing backlashes in the political arena.

There are also constraints on the financial resources which can be raised on the income side of the budget. Consideration must be given to the fact that excessively high rates of taxation may negatively affect incentives to work and produce, and in more extreme cases lead to a serious loss of business confidence.

User charges are an alternative form of financing welfare projects which became more popular as developing countries came increasingly under strain as a result of adjustment policies (Griffin and Knight, 1989). However, as Cornia insists, 'the potentially regressive nature of user charges should be emphasised, as in many developing countries, the need for health care, education etc. rarely coincides with the ability to pay for it' (1987b, p. 169). The evidence suggests that raising user charges leads to a reduction in the use of services by vulnerable people (ibid.). This has negative implications not only for the individuals concerned but for the productive potential of society as a whole.

It is important, however, to note that although financial limitations and the necessity to maintain macroeconomic balance impose hard constraints on economic policies, there is a great deal of flexibility within the design of macroeconomic strategies. For example, strategies aimed at encouraging the expansion of small-scale labour-intensive industries, the growth of urban employment and promoting development in rural areas, will have a more favourable impact on the poor than one which, for example, attempts to maximise capital accumulation in urban areas. Policies promoting the acquisition of skills are equally fundamental as they lay the basis for poor people to seize the opportunities provided by growth (World Bank, 1990, p. 51). Furthermore, the impact of macroeconomic policies on the poor can be substantially altered by a selective application of policies (e.g. in relation to import tariffs), through targeted programmes and by appropriate welfare spending (see below).

MICROECONOMIC PRIORITIES

Switching resources between public spending categories
Within the constraints set by the extent of the tax base, and hence the overall macroeconomic strategy, the size of the welfare budget is in the final analysis a function of how government prioritises welfare spending as an expenditure category. However, careful consideration of social, political and economic objectives needs to be undertaken at a host of different levels when the decision is made as to how much to reallocate from one category to another.

Economists sometimes attempt to calculate social rates of return when considering how to allocate state spending between the main sectors. The available evidence for developing countries suggests that 'the social rate of return tends to be highest for expenditures on education, training, rural infrastructure, health care and selected urban infrastructural works. Social rates of return, in contrast, are low or negative for expenditures on prestige infrastructure, defence and non-priority branches of public administration' (Cornia and Stewart, 1990, p. 12).

Although rates of return are a useful aid to decision-making, one should be cautious about over-emphasising them. There are numerous practical problems involved. One of the more important difficulties arises from the distinction between marginal and average returns. Allocation decisions should really be taken on marginal returns. But these are virtually impossible to calculate, with the result that serious errors can occur. For example, circumstances might arise where the marginal expenditure on secondary education gives the best return, even though the average rates of return to primary education exceed those of secondary education. In this case, additional expenditure should be switched to secondary education.

Despite this problem, and the limitations it imposes on decision-making, it is encouraging from a redistributive perspective to know that it generally pays to develop the primary dimensions of social spending, both in health and education. Targeting the poorest 40 per cent of society is justifiable on both ethical and economic grounds.

Another way of looking at the issue is to draw the distinction between welfare-oriented spending for consumption and for investment purposes. Where state spending is geared simply towards ensuring the basic survival of targeted individuals, the returns to society, in terms of increased capability for productive activity, tend to be less than they would be in the case of state spending in areas, such as education, which contribute significantly to the growth of 'human capital'.

In the interests of enhancing medium-term growth, the development strategy should prioritise policies which provide people with the capability for increased earning potential. This has implications for the beneficiaries of welfare policy. More investment-oriented programmes will tend to target younger groups, whereas consumption transfers are more neutral with respect to age, and might even go disproportionately to older people. Unless it can be shown that consumption transfers to older people are efficient and important ways of contributing to the survival and education of children, there is a strong argument for placing greater emphasis on the younger sections of society since a permanent solution to poverty requires that young people acquire sufficient skills.

The distinction between consumption and investment spending should, however, not be exaggerated as it is often a false one. Well-targeted social expenditure may help raise not only the consumption standards of the poor, but also productivity and overall output (Cornia and Stewart, 1990, p. 14). The case of old-age pensions illustrates the problem rather well. Although pensions are at first sight a consumption-oriented transfer, it has been claimed that they perform a vital role in the South African rural development chain, since a large proportion of the funds are devoted to supporting the young. Nevertheless, there are circumstances when welfare expenditures are primarily redistributive transfers and not justifiable in rates-of-return terms. Well-developed unemployment benefits might be an example. Clearly, for moral and economic reasons, a welfare policy should achieve a satisfactory balance between consumption and investment.

How much should go to welfare priorities?
It is difficult to come to grips with the concrete question of whether 'too little' or 'too much' is spent on welfare priorities as the question of need has to be balanced against that of resources and their alternative uses. Using international comparisons as a guide, Van der Berg has shown that South Africa's health performance is worse than expected, given the level of resources in terms of income and medical personnel (1990, pp. 73–4). As can be seen from Table 6.1, South Africa's quality of life indicators (life expectancy and infant mortality) are more in line with those of low-income countries, despite the fact that its per capita income is equivalent to that of upper-middle-income countries.

It is, however, difficult to conclude very much about policy from broad international comparisons. A certain minimum level of welfare expenditure is necessary before its impact on the poor becomes significant. As the World Bank notes, 'the countries that have succeeded in providing primary education and health care to the poor are those that have made adequate provision for the purpose in their budgets' (1990, p. 46). How much is 'adequate', of course, is difficult to know. As can be seen from Table 6.1, there is no clear relationship between the performance of life expectancy, infant mortality and the proportion of GNP spent on health.[2]

The more the state spends on health provision, the greater the chance of improving the quality of life of the poor. For example, in Costa Rica, where 5,4 per cent of GNP is spent on health, infant mortality is only 18. Compared with other lower-middle-income countries where just over half a per cent of GNP is spent on health, and infant mortality averages 57, this is a major achievement. Part of the reason for Costa Rica's success lies in its radical

Table 6.1. Comparative quality of life and economic indicators (1988)

Countries	GNP per capita ($)	Life expec- tancy	Infant morta- lity[a]	Govt exp as % GNP			Govt exp. as % of GNP
				Defence	Health	Educ	
Low income[b]	280	54	98	2,6	0,7	2,2	24,1
Sri Lanka	420	71	21	3,0	1,7	2,4	31,4
Indonesia	440	61	68	1,9	0,4	2,3	22,7
Lower middle	1 380	65	57	2,0	0,6	2,0	15,4
Brazil	2 160	65	61	1,0	2,4	1,2	25,1
Costa Rica	1 690	75	18	0,6	5,4	4,5	28,0
Botswana	1 010	67	41	6,2	3,8	9,2	50,9
Zimbabwe	650	63	49	6,3	2,9	8,5	38,7
Upper middle	3 240	68	42	–	–	–	–
Korea	3 600	70	24	4,3	0,3	3,0	15,7
Venezuela	3 250	70	35	1,3	2,2	4,3	21,8
Argentina	2 520	71	31	1,5	0,5	1,5	21,6
South Africa	2 290	61	70	4,3	3,2	6,1	33,1
High income	17 080	76	9	3,9	3,6	1,4	28,9
U.K.	12 810	75	9	4,7	5,1	0,8	37,6
Australia	12 340	76	9	2,6	2,8	2,1	28,7

Notes: [a] I.e. infant mortality per 1000 births. [b] Excluding China and India.
Sources: World Bank (1990), statistical tables numbers 1, 11, 28, 30; Statistical News
Release 'Expenditure by the General Government, 1982/83 – 1987/88', P9141, Central

re-orientation of health policy during the 1970s, which extended social security coverage from 39 per cent to 78 per cent of the population, decreased the number of hospitals from 51 to 37 while increasing the number of out-patient installations from 348 to 1 150 (Mosely and Jolly, 1987, p. 224). It is instructive to note that Costa Rica spends over twice the proportion of total spending on health and a sixth of the amount on defence as does South Africa.

However, it is possible to improve the quality of life of the poor without having to divert an enormous amount to health care. For example, Sri Lanka spends only 1,7 per cent of its GNP on health, yet infant mortality there is only 21. An essential ingredient of the Sri Lankan success story was of course its long commitment to Basic Needs policies and relatively high levels of spending on welfare (Stewart, 1985, p. 77). The achievement is nevertheless impressive, given that other low-income countries have an infant mortality rate of 98.

Just as relatively low spending on health is not always correlated with high infant mortality, a relatively higher percentage of social expenditure does not necessarily lead to relatively better quality of life indicators. The importance of variables other than government spending in determining quality of life, such as GDP per capita and income distribution, should not be forgotten. The fact that Costa Rica has a more equal distribution than many other countries in its income bracket, and has been pursuing a Basic Needs strategy since the 1950s, no doubt also helps explain why life expectancy and infant mortality rates are excellent.

South Africa's performance illustrates very clearly that relatively high levels of welfare spending do not necessarily lead to acceptable quality of life indicators. Unequal income distribution, other economic policies and the ways in which the particular welfare programmes are designed and implemented, are more important than their size when it comes to impact (Stewart, 1985; Cornia, 1989).

It is in this regard that South Africa's racially discriminatory policies are pertinent. For example, in 1986/7 education expenditure on black pupils was a mere 13 per cent of that on whites (Van der Berg, 1990, p. 79) while in 1990 black pensions were only 63 per cent of those of whites (Le Roux, 1990, p. 2). The full extent of the racial as well as regional bias in health expenditure is illustrated by the fact that per capita hospital-related expenditures were R38 for rural blacks, R159 for urban blacks and R238 for whites in 1986 (Van der Berg, 1990). It is obvious that inequitable state spending priorities have skewed the benefits of social spending away from blacks, and this must take much of the blame for the poor performance of South Africa's average quality of life indicators. For example, infant mortality for whites in South Africa has been estimated at 12 per thousand live births between 1981 and 1985, whereas the estimate for blacks ranges from 94 to 124 (World Bank, 1990, p. 37). Similarly the risk of contracting tuberculosis was 22 times greater for blacks in non-homeland areas than for whites, and 25 times greater in Transkei (ibid., pp. 37–8).

As noted earlier, South Africa spends a relatively large proportion of its GNP on social expenditures in comparison with the averages for other countries. However, as indicated by Table 6.1, there is a wide variation in the relative proportion of social spending. Recourse to international 'norms' of spending as a guide to budgetary allocation is less useful than examining ways in which macroeconomic and growth objectives can be made consistent with welfare priorities. Achieving a successful balance between reducing poverty through growth promotion and by redistributing through the budget is of overriding importance. For example, Brazil and Pakistan were able to reduce poverty through successful growth strategies, but owing to inadequate levels of social spending, maintained high levels of infant mortality. Conversely, Sri Lanka's impressive quality of life indicators have not been matched by significant increases in the incomes of the poor as growth has been inadequate. Indonesia and Malaysia, on the other hand, were able to increase the incomes of the poor by promoting the productive use of labour, while at the same time they increased the quality of life by means of social spending programmes (World Bank, 1990).

What welfare projects are appropriate?

The most obvious requirement of a welfare policy in South Africa is that it should not discriminate on the grounds of race and should be explicitly oriented towards the poor. As regards the former requirement, it is well known how biased state spending is towards whites. The evidence suggests that parity at current white levels is impossible and that a reduction in white standards will inevitably accompany a re-orientation of welfare spending towards the poor (Van der Berg, 1990).

Another equally important requirement of a welfare policy is that it be efficient and effective. Given that the provision of primary health care has had a significant impact on the health of the poor in many developing countries (World Bank, 1990, pp. 74–5) and that low-cost policies have over the past 10–15 years proved to be very successful at improving health and nutrition, even in adverse economic environments (Cornia, 1989, p. 160), it is likely that appropriately designed policies could achieve significant gains in South Africa at affordable costs.

HEALTH

The evidence from developing countries suggests that significant improvements in the health of the poor can be achieved if there is a lasting and consistent emphasis on preventive measures and basic curative care (World Bank, 1990, chapter 5; Cornia, 1990). The importance of such measures is illustrated by the fact that where cutbacks in basic health expenditure occurred as part of structural adjustment programmes, the consequences in terms of health indicators became visible very rapidly (Pinstrup-Andersen *et al.*, 1987, pp. 73–83). It is now accepted that primary health care has a far greater social rate of return than hospital care (Cornia and Stewart, 1990, p. 15).

Cornia lists the main components of low-cost preventive and curative policies that have been followed with great success in certain developing countries:

(a) A simple pregnancy management programme consisting of periodic check-ups for pregnant women, supplementary feeding for malnourished mothers, vaccination against tetanus and training of traditional birth attendants;

(b) Oral rehydration therapy (ORT), which is the most appropriate treatment for most digestive tract infections, while improvements in water supply and sanitation and health education are the best forms of prevention. ORT consists of the administration of a simple mix of salt, sugar and boiled water, and can stop the dehydration which kills an estimated 5 million young children a year;

(c) Immunisation, providing full protection to children against the six communicable diseases, measles, meningitis, whooping cough, diphtheria, TBC and poliomyelitis, and against tetanus neonatorum;

(d) An essential drug programme, covering about 15-20 basic products, provides efficient treatment (at the level of primary health care) to many health problems, including infectious diseases and insect-borne diseases. The bulk purchase of generic drugs, reliance on the communities for their transport and the use of village health posts for their distribution are important elements of the programme...

Such an approach aims at providing basic care to all citizens through a three-tier health system manned at the first level by village health workers and paraprofessionals. It places strong emphasis on community involvement, preventive action, the broadening of health interventions so as to include basic education, proper nutrition, safe water and sanitation (1989, pp. 166–7).

The above policies are of course extremely basic. The important point is that this bottom line needs to be extended to *all* before consideration is given to upgrading the health system. It is difficult to pinpoint how much South Africa spends on curative and preventive health – a task made even more difficult than usual by the existence of 14 Departments of Health and the myriad of channels through which health spending is directed. However, the Brown Commission (1986) has estimated that less than 5 per cent of total public health spending in South Africa is directed towards preventive medicine. Whatever the details, there is little doubt though that an insufficient proportion of health resources is being channelled in that direction, though one can never say with any great clarity what the proportion ought to be.

Perhaps the most important criticism of the way in which the health budget is spent in South Africa is that there seems to be no rational basis for allocating spending. Rather than expenditure being a function of need, it appears to be dominated by the demands of existing bureaucracies and a preference on the part of medical personnel for a more capital-intensive curative approach.[3] For example, of the 82 per cent of health spending allocated to non-homeland areas in South Africa, 76 per cent goes to the provincial administrations (which administer curative, hospital-centred health services), 18 per cent to the Department of National Health, 4 per cent to the tricameral structures and only 2 per cent to local government (McIntyre, 1990, p. 15). As most primary health care occurs within the ambit of local government, it is clear that very little is allocated in South Africa to primary health care. According to Donaldson, claims on curative care can always be presented as a matter of urgency; 'the failure of government to commit sufficient resources to preventive services is in part a consequence of the failure to put in place sufficiently rigorous rationing and pricing rules governing access and entitlement to curative services' (1990, p. 18). The duplication of administrative structures has made it even more difficult to develop coherent health norms.

Clearly the way in which spending is planned and allocated is in need of fundamental restructuring, with a more focussed orientation towards the poor and the provision of basic health care in rural areas and urban informal settlements. Devising such a health programme is obviously beyond the authors' abilities. However, it is a useful exercise to point to the low-cost solutions that have been tried and tested elsewhere in the world. Similar programmes are within reach of South Africa's existing budgetary resources.

After surveying the available evidence of the cost of health care projects, Cornia concludes that 'comprehensive and high-impact primary health care services can be provided at a cost of $2–$5 per capita per year' (1989, p. 174).[4] If we take the $5 estimate for the provision of primary health services, the rand equivalent would be approximately R12,50. Assuming a population of 38 million this implies an expenditure of about R475 million, i.e. less than one-tenth of the R7,4 billion allocated to health spending in 1989/90. Although these figures are only guesstimates, the point is simply that low-cost primary health care provision is possible if international experience is anything to go by. For example, an analysis of a comprehensive programme in Indonesia covering 9 million children and including growth monitoring, supplementary feeding for energy and micro-nutrients, immunisation, oral rehydration, training of midwives and family planning, estimated a yearly average cost per child under the age of 5 to be $11–$12, and per head of population to be $2 (Cornia, 1989, p. 171).

Of course, once personnel and capital formation costs are included in the costing of primary health services, the estimate of per capita cost will rise significantly. This could be the most expensive part of the process of upgrading the quality of primary health care. It is also worth noting that the existing system of primary health care is fairly well developed in some areas of South Africa. Certainly as far as the provision of clinics is concerned, the infrastructure is substantially in place for the development of an effective primary health care programme. However, as can be seen in Table 6.2, the ratio of population per clinic is extremely uneven.

Table 6.2. Health indicators for selected 'homeland' areas

	Per capita expenditure on health (1985)	Population per clinic	Population per nurse	Population per doctor
Bophuthatswana	83	11 230	651	16 421
Ciskei	46	7 979	224	3 989
Transkei	41	13 455	537	11 827
Venda	46	9 200	603	24 210

Source: Development Bank of Southern Africa (1987).

It is clear that Transkei has an inadequate number of clinics whereas Ciskei's record is impressive. Interestingly, Ciskei spends a relatively low amount per capita on health, yet is able to finance a significantly greater number of clinics, doctors and nurses per head of population. This points to the potential for efficiency gains in reallocating health expenditure.

Although there is room for re-orienting existing public health resources, it might not be so easy to switch them from tertiary to primary health. Some increase in overall expenditure, which could be clawed back by cutting the existing subsidies going towards the private health sector, may be necessary. A good-quality primary health care programme might also produce some savings by reducing pressure on more expensive curative facilities. It is worth stressing that those primary health care projects which have been successful have relied heavily on social mobilisation and community participation rather than the expansion of the state health bureaucracy. This, according to Cornia, 'results in better organised, self-reliant and dynamic communities with greater collective bargaining power and with an increased ability to take advantage of economic and political opportunities' (1989, pp. 184–5).

Primary health care is clearly vital from the perspective of the poor and is the essential instrument for improving quality of life indicators. Programmes of this nature are comfortably within South Africa's reach and should enjoy priority. The next level of health care, which involves the general practitioner or family care clinics, is also relevant to alleviating the health problems of the poor. The options facing South Africa in this arena are complex and under-researched. It is perhaps in this sphere where a switch in resources from tertiary to lower levels of health care might be most readily accomplished. Getting the correct balance between preventive and curative health spending and between the mix of public and private-sector health provision involves tough and awkward decisions. Such questions are beyond the scope of this chapter.

NUTRITION INTERVENTIONS

The available evidence concerning nutritional status in South Africa suggests that malnutrition is rife (see Wilson and Ramphele, 1989, ch. 5). One study estimated that 'approximately a third of black, coloured and Asian children below the age of 14 years are underfed and stunted for their age' (Hanson, 1984, p. 7). Malnutrition not only stunts growth, and thus also the capacity for productive employment as an adult, but also makes children far more susceptible to killer diseases such as gastroenteritis and pneumonia (Wilson and Ramphele, 1989, p. 109).

Although malnutrition is primarily a function of the household's access to income, some improvement in the nutritional status of the poor can be made by means of supplementary feeding schemes, subsidies on basic foodstuffs, targeted food aid (for example through the distribution of food coupons to target groups) and micro-nutrient supplementation.

The use of subsidies has been criticised because most of it goes on the rich as they spend more on food. However, as the poor spend a higher percentage of their income on food, cutting food subsidies has adverse distributional consequences. A rule of thumb regarding subsidies might be to subsidise only inferior goods (Laraki, 1989, p. 405), i.e. items such as maize and bread. It might also be the easiest form of food aid to administer.

Targeted food aid is another possibility, and international evidence suggests that supplementary feeding of children and pregnant and lactating women has substantial long-run beneficial effects on health status and productivity (Cornia, 1989). According to Cornia and Stewart's survey of the evidence, 'child feeding and food stamps programmes are more equitable and efficient than urban food subsidies' (1990, p. 15). However, for these to work effectively, adequate administrative structures need to be put in place. Furthermore, appropriate and effective ways of identifying the target population must be ascertained. In this respect, the evidence suggests that 'Targeting is distributionally and administratively more effective when it is done by some objective criteria such as geography (the poorest areas), commodity (subsidising 'inferior foods' not consumed by the rich), easily identifiable population groups (pregnant women and young children), season, or employment in food-for-work schemes (with real wages set so as to attract only the really poor). It is the least effective when done by means-testing and earmarking of individuals' (Cornia and Stewart, 1990, pp. 15–16).

As regards micro-nutrient deficiencies, it is now possible to fortify a country's salt supply with iron and iodine. Alternatively, intramuscular injections of iodised oil can provide protection for up to 5 years (Cornia, 1989, p. 168). The costs of such supplementation are very low. According to a 1987 study, vitamin A capsules cost $0,10 per person per year, iodising salt costs $0,05 and providing iron by fortification of salt or centrally processed grains costs between $0,05 and $0,09 per person per year (Berg, 1987). Such low-cost micro-nutrient supplementation has been found to affect productivity and attention span significantly (Cornia, 1989, pp. 179–80). For this reason, there is little tension between the goals of welfare spending for consumption and investment purposes.

Other nutritional interventions which are worth examining include school-feeding schemes in targeted areas. In the 1990 illustrative budget of the Democratic Party, an estimate of R1,69 million was put forward as a cost of feeding needy primary school students. This calculation assumes 2,1 million children in need and a cost per child of R15–R16 per month.[5] Similar calculations were made by the Democratic Party (on the basis of Operation Hunger estimates) for the costs of feeding infants and pre-school children in need. The total estimates were R300 million and R169 million respectively. However, given the incompetence of educational bureaucracies in black areas, one would need to spend a great deal more on either improving existing structures or generating new ones, if school feeding is going to effectively reach those most in need.

EMPLOYMENT

For all the potential that health and nutritional interventions may have to improve the quality of life of the poor, it cannot be over-stressed that the most important way of alleviating poverty is to create income-earning opportunities for the poor. A special employment programme (SEP) of some sort should thus be high on any anti-poverty agenda. The activities involved might include road and dam building, housing construction, environmental protection, etc.

It is important to be clear about the purpose of SEPs. The main goal is to create a source of income for poor households. Other goals which might be relevant include providing training, establishing physical infrastructure and supplying social services. These different goals may sometimes be at odds with one another, and confusion over the main priority of SEPs often lies at the root of disappointments with their performance. For instance, the people who are most in need of employment under a poverty scheme are not necessarily physically able or sufficiently skilled to provide the most appropriate labour input for an infrastructural project. An emphasis on poverty alleviation may also impose expenditure norms and timing constraints which are not desirable from a long-term development perspective.

The world-wide trend in the 1970s and early 1980s has been towards emphasising considerations of economic viability and development in the design of SEPs. This is to some extent the result of the severe fiscal pressures that governments began to encounter, which made it more difficult for them to address poverty and equity issues. The disenchantment with relief schemes was, however, also due to the often inferior quality of the assets generated by short-term employment-oriented programmes. For this reason, it has been argued that longer-term employment and development objectives should be prioritised (Freedman, 1990, p. 169).

In the South African context, Abedian and Standish (1986, 1989) have proposed an extensive public works programme which emphasises the need to integrate the different objectives of SEPs. For them, the broader developmental goals are as important as the immediate poverty-relief aspect. They are therefore explicitly opposed to schemes which offer notional jobs at minimal wages. They also argue at length in favour of reducing inefficiencies and maximising the longer-term development objectives of such programmes. This implies careful planning, systematic organisation and a high level of government commitment.

It is, however, unclear whether South Africa has the administrative capacity to implement programmes of the quality and scale advocated by Abedian and Standish. Moreover, they recommend that the wage level satisfy at least the Household Subsistence Level. This amounts to a wage in 1990 prices of approximately R450 in rural areas and R630 in urban areas, and means that the proposal is unaffordable. For instance, assuming a labour cost component of 60 per cent, a scheme employing one million people, equally split between urban and rural areas, will cost in the region of R9 billion at 1990 prices. This is some 4 per cent of GDP and is way beyond South Africa's means.

At the same time, one has to acknowledge the intrinsic merits of many of the concrete programmes proposed by Abedian and Standish. They suggest that most of the effort in the urban areas should be concentrated on providing housing and residential infrastructure. Both of these are widely viewed as national priorities. By the same token, one cannot fault the principles behind their recommendations for rural development projects.

The important question here, though, is whether one should endeavour to incorporate all of these programmes under the rubric of SEPs. If the primary objective of an SEP is to relieve poverty and to redistribute income towards specific groups, then one should not subordinate this aim to those of more general development initiatives. The equity issue is so easily compromised in standard cost-benefit analysis as a result of technical and planning requirements.

This does not mean that poverty-oriented SEPs must necessarily have negligible long-run returns. In fact, Stewart maintains that many of these schemes lead to an improvement in the incomes of target groups in the long run, sometimes of such magnitude that they exceed the short-run effects (1987b, p. 205). It all depends on whether development agencies or community organisations make imaginative use of the resources at their disposal. Nevertheless, it is essential to be clear about priorities, especially in the event of conflicting objectives.

The South African R600 million employment scheme that was introduced during the recession of 1985–6 illustrates some of the dilemmas rather well (Barker, 1986; Viljoen et al., 1987). The scheme concentrated very much on providing relief employment, and was even linked to the idea of a meal a day for destitute families. However, the speed with which the programme was introduced meant that many of the projects were relatively unproductive. Some of these problems might have been resolved if the programme had been allowed to continue and if development agencies had had more time for planning. Even so, the transfers provided by the project were meaningful, and the strong demand for places on the scheme, particularly in the rural areas, must give some indication of the need for such poverty-relief programmes.

The gaps in South Africa's welfare net are of such magnitude that serious consideration should be given to introducing employment programmes which specifically address poverty and cater for some of the most vulnerable groups. Such a scheme need not be viewed as a substitute for conventional development projects. The latter can be justified without reference to short-term employment benefits. There is also no reason why an SEP should not be used in support of long-run aims, provided these do not push the shorter-term anti-poverty objective into the background.

The World Bank (1990) has come out explicitly in favour of SEPs as instruments of welfare policy. The report maintains that SEPs tend to be cost-effective relief measures since the wage level can be used to screen out the non-poor. Only poor people are willing to work for low wages. In this way one might reduce the administrative costs and disincentive effects of welfare programmes which rely on means-testing and contingent criteria for allocating welfare benefits. This does not mean that SEPs do not incur comparable costs. They require administrative input on a scale similar to other welfare programmes. Furthermore, they obviously also have an opportunity cost in terms of time which could have been spent looking for work or engaging in other productive activities. These negative effects are, however, likely to be less severe than for transfer programmes based on means-testing.

On the administrative side, SEPs offer the advantage that they can draw on locally based structures, especially if the output is of benefit to the communities involved. While, as stressed above, these developmental benefits should not be the driving force behind SEPs, they are nevertheless distinctive of such an approach to welfare delivery. The World Bank (1990) also argues that many SEPs have been relatively successful in reaching the most appropriate target groups. But this usually requires a strong commitment towards drawing the poorest into the ambit of these schemes. Employment guarantees have been quite effective in this regard and, in addition, seem to provide an automatic mechanism for redistributing incomes towards areas where the demand for work is greatest. The Maharashtra Employment Guarantee Scheme in India has been run successfully on this basis for many years.[6]

The costs of a fairly extensive poverty-oriented SEP for South Africa need not be prohibitive. If, for example, 500 000 people were employed at a wage of R175 per month – which is the old-age pension for Africans and is slightly more than one half of the cash and in-kind wage of the average urban female domestic worker – and labour costs were held at 60 per cent of total costs (which is an internationally accepted norm), then the total bill would be in the region of R1,76 billion per annum, which is well below 1 per cent of GDP. Even a programme accommodating a million people could be considered, provided the wage was held sufficiently low. Donaldsons's finding that in the case of partially subsidised community-controlled projects in Transkei the wage was typically set below the norms suggested by the authorities, is of interest in this context (1987, p. 54).

Focussing on the need for large-scale low-wage projects means that one is implicitly supporting policies which extend rather than deepen the welfare safety net in South Africa. We argue that additional welfare instruments should be created in order to extend the welfare net to more people. There are hard choices to be made in every category of spending. In the interests of targeting as many of the poor as possible, it is probable that SEPs offering low wages to many people are preferable to better-paying programmes with limited employment effects, or even increased pension pay-outs to those households lucky enough to have access to a pensioner.

For the welfare safety net to be broadened to as many poor as possible, it is important that projects and policies are correctly targeted. Because the poor tend to be concentrated in rural areas, in female-headed households, there is a clear need for SEPs to be generated in rural areas and in ways that promote the participation of women. Other areas which would benefit particularly from SEPs include squatter settlements and areas occupied by more recent urban immigrants.

CONCLUSION

The last three sections indicated that low-cost but effective welfare programmes are possible and within reach. However, such programmes tend to be fairly marginal aspects of state spending. When one looks at the issue of welfare-oriented state spending at a broader level, the old economic problem of scarce resources and hard choices between competing claims comes immediately to the fore. In this respect, the point was made early on in the chapter that considerations such as prioritising spending on investment in people (rather than spending for consumption) and ensuring high social rates of return to spending in the medium term, need to be taken very seriously when designing the appropriate mix of welfare policies.

If growth is to be encouraged and sustained, then welfare spending on education and training must receive a very high priority. The evidence suggests that spending on primary education (which manifests a far greater social rate of return than tertiary education – Cornia and Stewart, 1990, p. 15), and on the promotion of industrial capabilities (Lall, 1989), is particularly important. Although choices have to be made between different welfare policies, there are complementarities involved as well. For example, it has been demonstrated that investing resources in the education of women has positive implications for the health and nutrition of children (Cornia, 1987b).

What is needed is a carefully thought-out plan to guide the allocation of state spending to growth and welfare priorities. This involves political choices, economic analysis of costs and benefits, and above all an understanding of who are the poor and the nature of their needs. Poverty has different faces in different regions (Wilson and Ramphele, 1989) and very different coping mechanisms are evident. More detailed understanding is necessary before policies can be designed.

7

Options for employment creation

ANDRÉ ROUX

The number of formal sector jobs in the South African economy has virtually stopped expanding. It appears that fewer than one-tenth of the new labour market entrants each year manage to find a formal sector job. This dismal state of affairs is well understood by ordinary people. A recent survey among township residents found that unemployment is ranked as the most serious problem confronting the country (Whittle, 1990).

The causes of unemployment in South Africa have several distinct dimensions. The lack of economic growth is at the heart of the problem, and a return to respectable levels of growth is the only sure way of addressing the issue. There are, nevertheless, other factors which seem to aggravate the problem. These are briefly analysed below. The remainder of the chapter evaluates some of the policies which might be used to promote job creation. The interaction between possible growth scenarios and employment is first considered. This is followed by a discussion of measures for dealing with factor price distortions and labour market imperfections. The chapter concludes with an assessment of interventions applicable to specific sectors of the economy.

It is important to recognise at the outset that there is a worthwhile distinction to be made between growth strategies and employment policies. This is not always appreciated in the literature, with the result that discussions on employment creation often deteriorate into debates about growth strategies. The aims of this chapter are more modest. It considers what policies might be introduced to ensure that the pattern of growth is employment-intensive. No attempt is made, however, to develop a set of growth-promoting policies *per se*.

Extent of unemployment
South Africa's disastrous employment record is evident from Table 7.1. This oft-quoted table compares the trend in the number of formal-sector employment opportunities with the size of the potential workforce (assumed to consist of 100 per cent of the male and 50 per cent of the female population

between the ages of 20 and 64).

Table 7.1.   Workforce and formal employment, 1946–88: annual totals (x 1000)

Year	Formal employment	Work force	Without formal work	
			Number	Percent
1946	3 399	4 447	1 048	23,6
1950	3 790	4 902	1 112	22,7
1955	4 366	5 539	1 173	21,2
1960	4 652	6 258	1 606	25,7
1965	5 440	7 124	1 684	23,6
1970	6 164	8 110	1 946	24,0
1975	6 942	9 356	2 414	25,8
1980	7 391	10 794	3 403	31,5
1985	7 692	12 346	4 654	37,7
1986	7 615	12 691	5 076	40,0
1987	7 712	13 047	5 335	40,1
1988	7 781	13 412	5 631	42,0

Source: Roukens de Lange (1989), Ligthelm and Kritzinger-Van Niekerk (1990).

In the 1950s and 1960s the percentage of the workforce without formal-sector employment tended to fluctuate within a band in the low twenties (with perhaps a slight hint of an upward trend). The mid-1970s saw a dramatic change in the trend, with the estimated number of people in the workforce without formal jobs rising from around 2 million to more than 5 million in the late 1980s. Table 7.2 illustrates even more vividly the failure of the formal sector to absorb the workforce. Very few new jobs were created during the 1980s. The percentage of the annual net additions to the workforce who were drawn into the formal sector decreased from 91,3 per cent in the early 1960s to a paltry 8,5 per cent in the late 1980s.

Table 7.2. Workforce and formal employment, 1946–88: average annual increase (x 1000)

Year	Formal employment	Work force	Percentage absorbed
1946–50	98	114	86,0
1950–55	115	127	90,6
1955–60	57	144	39,8
1960–65	158	173	91,3
1965–70	145	197	73,6
1970–75	156	249	62,7
1975–80	90	288	31,3
1980–85	60	310	19,4
1985–88	30	355	8,5

Adapted from: Ligthelm and Kritzinger-Van Niekerk (1990).

What about unemployment? A decrease in the number of workers being absorbed into the formal sector does not imply an equivalent increase in open unemployment. The unemployment rate is influenced by other variables as well. Two of these are particularly relevant here. They are the proportion of the workforce (as defined above) who are economically active in the sense of being keen to find work under current conditions, and the level of employment in the informal and subsistence sectors. Both of these variables are difficult to define and measure, with the result that any estimate of the level of unemployment is somewhat arbitrary.

The current controversy over the size of the informal sector illustrates the problem. The issue was recently surveyed by Van der Berg (1990). He observes that estimates of employment in the informal sector range from a liberal 29 per cent to a conservative 10 per cent of the labour force. A comprehensive attempt at surveying the size of the sector was recently undertaken by the Central Statistical Services (CSS). Using their 1989 figures, and adjusting for the fact that their statistics exclude the TBVC areas (TBVC rates are assumed to be proportional to those in the self-governing territories), one arrives at an estimate for employment in the informal sector of 3,5 million. Not all of these people are, however, part of the labour force. If full-time housewives and scholars are excluded from the CSS figure then the contribution of the informal sector drops to 2,2 million, or 15,8 per cent of the workforce. In any event, whatever the specific details, it is clear that the informal sector plays a significant role in reducing the level of open unemployment.

A related dispute about the size of the labour force took place when the first estimates of unemployment were produced and it became apparent that South Africa was suffering from an escalating unemployment rate. Since no unambiguous operational definition of the labour force exists, it is logically feasible for an adherent to the efficient labour market perspective to argue that estimates of high unemployment largely reflect high inactivity levels. To illustrate the problem, consider a woman who lives in the homelands. The only jobs which are open to her will probably require long-distance migration. But she is likely to be unable to enter these markets because of domestic responsibilities. Should one then classify her as unemployed or as a housewife who is not part of the labour force?

The problems mentioned above cannot be settled unambiguously. As South African economists have realised, any attempt to measure the absolute level of unemployment must necessarily be of limited value. It is the trend that is really important. But for the record, using the official Current Population Survey estimates of unemployment, which are of course problematic in their own right, and making certain obvious assumptions about the usual gaps in their information (no estimates for TBVC countries or for whites), one arrives at a national unemployment figure of 14,2 per cent for June 1987 (the first time the new CPS surveys were introduced).

Some idea of the characteristics of the unemployed can be gleaned from

Table 7.3. Profile of the labour force and the unemployed, 1987 (Africans)

		Percentage distribution Labour force	Unemployed	Unemployment rate
Sex:	Male	64,2	35,8	12,6
	Female	35,8	53,3	25,8
Age:	Below 25	23,8	34,6	25,2
	25–34	32,6	34,9	18,5
	Above 34	43,6	30,6	12,1
Education:	Below Std 3	41,3	36,1	15,1
	Std 4–7	44,4	46,8	18,2
	Above Std 4	14,3	17,1	20,7
Region:	Metropolitan	33,7	34,3	17,6
	Towns	8,4	7,4	15,4
	Farms	22,4	7,1	5,5
	Homelands	35,6	51,1	24,9

Source: Data from the Current Population Survey of June 1987, recorded in *South African Labour Statistics 1988*.

Table 7.3. The profile of the unemployed in South Africa is not too dissimilar from those found elsewhere in the world. The unemployment rates for females and the young are almost twice as large as the rates for males and older workers. There are also major spatial differences in unemployment, especially in the case of the rural areas; the very high rate in the homelands contrasts sharply with the low figure for white-owned farms. The demographic controls of the past forced Africans out of the latter areas and into the former. Finally, the table indicates a negative correlation between education and unemployment. Although the particular result depicted in the table is largely due to the association between age and education, there is evidence that such a negative correlation exists irrespective of age.

Causes of unemployment

Although the early 1980s saw a vigorous debate on the nature of unemployment in South Africa, it is now generally accepted that the post-1970 decline in the rate of economic growth is the most important single factor underlying

Table 7.4. Employment and output growth, 1946–87

	1948–60	1960–70	1970–81	1981–87
Average annual growth rates:				
(1) Real output	4,3	5,7	3,5	0,8
(2) Formal employment	2,2	2,6	1,6	0,2
Elasticity of employment with respect to output = (2)/(1)	0,51	0,46	0,46	0,25

Source: Terence Moll (1989).

the rising unemployment rate. The table above illustrates the close association that exists between output growth and formal-sector employment growth.

The other component of the conventional wisdom about unemployment concerns factor prices. There is evidence that the increase in unemployment has been accompanied by excessive capital deepening throughout the economy. Table 7.5 depicts the considerable acceleration in the rate of growth of the capital–labour ratio that took place between 1970 and 1986.

Table 7.5. Growth of capital–labour ratios, 1960–86

| Sector | Average annual growth rate | | |
	1960–70	1970–80	1980–86
Agriculture	1,47	5,55	2,88
Mining	0,88	5,34	4,93
Manufacturing	3,37	5,17	4.29
Construction	5,27	7,54	1,95
Trade	–0,36	2,49	2.76
Transport	–0,27	3,91	4,64
Total	2,83	4,58	3.92

Adapted from: Biggs (1981) and National Productivity Institute (1990)

The trend towards capital intensity is counter-intuitive. Rising unemployment ought to have been associated with a drop in the relative price for labour and hence a decline in the growth of the capital–labour ratio. The actual trend, however, cannot be dismissed since the same pattern repeats itself across various sectors of the formal economy. The generality of the trend lends credence to the suggestion that distortions to factor prices have played a role in reducing the capacity of the economy to absorb labour (Biggs, 1981). The decline in the responsiveness of employment to increases in the output of the economy shown in Table 7.4 is also consistent with this view.[1] It is widely believed that policies which arbitrarily reduce the costs of capital relative to labour are to some extent responsible for these trends. Included in the usual list are interest rate policies, tax concessions, overvalued exchange rates, regulations and import-substitution industrialisation. Interest rates may be particularly significant as real interest rates have been largely negative since the early 1970s.

Further support for the factor price distortion hypothesis comes from the post-1986 trend in the capital–labour ratio. The recent report of the National Productivity Institute (1990) suggests that rapid capital deepening may have come to a sudden end in 1986. It would appear that the shift towards positive interest rates has brought about a sharp decline in the rate of growth of the capital–labour ratio.

The behaviour of real wages is also crucial. Although one should guard against assigning causal significance to real wages in explaining unemployment, there is now a considerable body of empirical evidence which suggests that the behaviour of nominal wages is related to the persistence of unemployment in many OECD economies (Bean *et al.*, 1986; Freeman, 1988). Both a decline in the rate of growth of output and a rise in the rate of growth of the capital–labour ratio can only affect unemployment indirectly, i.e. through their direct impact on the rate of growth of the demand for labour. For unemployment to emerge, even though the triggering mechanism might be a drop in the demand for labour at each wage, requires a sluggish response on the part of wages to changes in the demand for labour.

This is, of course, a controversial position. Nevertheless, there is a great deal of casual evidence that suggests that many unemployed workers would be prepared to take work at wage levels significantly below current formal sector wages. The growth of the informal sector is partly also a reflection of this state of affairs. But this is exactly what it means to say that formal sector wages exceed their market-clearing levels. However, such a conclusion immediately begs the question: why do formal sector wages not drop in response to what appears to be an excess supply of labour? Why, for instance, do unemployed workers not undercut the wages of their employed comrades?

A plethora of explanations for labour market failure have emerged in recent years. To begin with, there are theories, such as the implicit contract models, which concentrate on explaining nominal wage inflexibility. Contracts are a possible source of rigidity since wages are not able to adjust while employment and wage contracts, including implicit ones, are in force. Although these theories provide a convincing account of wage rigidity in the short run, it is not clear why contracts should lead to long-term deviations of wages from their market-clearing levels. A more promising set of explanations for labour market failure is derived from the efficiency wage hypothesis. The real wage may be positively related to profitability over a certain range owing to a variety of circumstances, including nutrition, job turnover costs, and worker morale. Firms may then have an incentive to set wages above their equilibrium levels, resulting in unemployment, and possibly excessive capital deepening in the long run.

Monopolistic behaviour on the part of trade unions and established workers is another source of market failure. It is a well-established empirical fact that unionisation has a positive impact on wage levels. But, as the so-called insider–outsider models illustrate, even in the absence of unions, it is possible for an established workforce to capture some of the rents associated with turnover costs and to prevent underbidding by unemployed workers (Lindbeck and Snower, 1986, 1988). Some hysteresis models of unemployment, which attempt to explain why current levels of unemployment seem to be a function of past levels of unemployment, also focus on the control which insiders are able to exercise over wage levels (Blanchard and Summers, 1988).

The applicability of these models to the South African labour market is an unresolved issue. An investigation by Peter Moll (1990) of wage dispersion across industries tends to undermine the empirical basis for efficiency wages, but without disproving their existence. The same author (1991a) finds that the wage differential between unionised and non-unionised workers is relatively small. These studies suggest that evidence of wage inflexibility in the South African economy would have to be sought elsewhere. A good deal of additional empirical work needs to be done before these conclusions can be accepted. Economists therefore have to concede that some of the most fundamental questions about unemployment in South Africa still remain unanswered.

In conclusion, one should note certain additional characteristics of the South African labour markets which exacerbate the extent of labour market frictions. Some of these are unique, or at least different from those found in advanced countries. The effects of past controls over labour mobility are frequently mentioned in this regard. These may have distorted the behaviour of homeland residents and produced a degree of so-called wait unemployment, and certainly a mismatch between the location of the unemployed and employment opportunities. A variety of other factors, including poverty, cumulative inertia, labour market withdrawal, exclusion from search networks and inadequate information, are all present in South African labour markets, and make it more difficult for certain segments of the labour force to search effectively for work. In some markets these factors will have shielded formal sector workers from competition by the unemployed.

Employment and growth

At the most general level it is obvious that any employment policy must be situated within the context of an economic growth strategy. As is clear from the previous discussion, only growth can provide a satisfactory resolution to the unemployment problem. Although this obvious truth is not always emphasised by everyone, there is broad acceptance that employment is essentially a derivative of economic growth.

Recognising that growth is ultimately vital to solving the unemployment problem does not mean that employment policies should focus exclusively on questions of growth. Policies which maximise the rate of growth of output will not necessarily do the same for employment. To achieve more rapid employment growth might require additional interventions, even to the point where it may be necessary to introduce measures aimed at facilitating a different, and possibly slower, pattern of output growth. In choosing between growth-promoting policies one has to be sensitive to the labour intensity of alternative growth paths. It is for this reason that employment strategies are legitimate components of growth strategies.

A surprising degree of consensus about the broad outlines of a growth–employment strategy emerged during 1990. The three components of government strategy consisted of (a) restructuring the modern economy to improve its productivity, international competitiveness and income-generating capacity; (b) a process of inward industrialisation, whereby labour-intensive production is stimulated as a result of changes in income distribution and urbanisation; and (c) rural development based on proper utilisation of existing resource endowments (Calitz, 1990, p. 13). Similarly, the policy document of the South African Chamber of Business states that the potential of inward industrialisation, using a public housing provision programme to provide jobs and training, should be exploited in order to ensure adequate employment opportunities (SACOB, 1990, p. 18). It should, however, also be noted that SACOB's overarching commitment to growth is revealed by the rider which was added to the above passage: 'it must also be borne in mind that South Africa has to remain globally competitive.' The ANC's discussion document covers similar ground, although in their case, the emphasis seems to be directed more towards inward industrialisation. It states that the first priority of industrial planning should be to ensure that adequate productive capacity emerges to meet the new demands for basic needs created by redistribution. The document proceeds to argue that industrial policies should also aim at transforming imbalances between blacks and whites, men and women, and urban and rural areas, and that the dependence of manufacturing on imports has to be overcome by reducing import intensities and increasing exports. The ANC also mentions specifically that a housing public works programme should be used to promote job creation (ANC, 1990, p. 8).

The apparent consensus revealed by the above passages is deceptive. While there is consensus that inward industrialisation should be an integral component of any employment strategy, there are disagreements about its role in relation to economic growth. Both the government and business appear to be more committed to an export-orientation than the ANC. They place much greater emphasis on the need to improve productivity and competitiveness, and assign priority to this component of their strategies. The ANC, on the other hand, adheres to a broader interpretation of inward industrialisation than that of the present government, and certainly views it as more than a housing programme, as appears to be the case in the SACOB document.

Part of the problem is that inward industrialisation is not precisely defined. For Lombard, who first introduced the term in 1985, inward industrialisation is the process that would arise if the poor and the unemployed were placed in a position where they could earn and consume on a much larger scale (Lombard, 1988, p. 1). He argued that an expansion in the incomes of the poorer – but more rapidly growing – component of the population was a precondition for further economic growth in South Africa. Lombard went on to argue that deregulation, realistic factor prices and manpower development were necessary to trigger this release of economic potential. In terms of this interpretation, inward industrialisation requires less, not more, state intervention.

A somewhat different, although by no means inconsistent, approach to inward industrialisation was proposed by Dreyer and Brand (1986), who were the first to postulate a connection between income redistribution and urbanisation, on the one hand, and employment creation and growth, on the other. With the aid of an input–output analysis they showed that urbanisation and redistribution would tend to favour the more employment-intensive and less import-intensive sectors of the economy. This, then, amounted to a suggestion that would at once bring relief to the most serious constraints on growth, namely the balance of payments and excessive capital deepening. The opportunities which housing presented as an instrument to initiate the process were subsequently recognised, thus providing a rationale for more active intervention by the government.

In evaluating the role of inward industrialisation it is useful to distinguish between its possible growth effects and its employment-oriented aspects. There is some disagreement on this issue. In the ANC's discussion document, inward industrialisation is primarily perceived as a growth strategy. Lombard also saw a significant growth-generative role for inward industrialisation. The dominant position in government, however, foresees a more limited purpose. For them, inward industrialisation is essentially the employment-creating component of their strategy. As Croeser, Director-General of Finance, put it: 'in the South African case the special appeal of the process lies in its low import propensity on the one hand and its high labour intensity on the other' (Croeser, 1990, p. 9).

It is beyond the scope of this chapter to discuss the merits of inward industrialisation as a growth strategy. Nevertheless one cannot be certain that the virtuous circle foreseen by proponents of the process would necessarily occur. For the moment it is more important to consider whether inward industrialisation could, either as a primary or secondary growth strategy, have a substantial impact on employment. One of the shortcomings of evaluations of inward industrialisation as an employment-creation policy is that no-one has made any attempt to assess the net employment effects of the programme. These will probably be positive. There is no doubt that the construction sector is more labour-intensive than most of the other sectors of the economy. A shift towards construction would therefore raise the employment associated with each unit of output.

It is, however, not clear that the magnitude of this shift would be significant. The input–output estimates of Roukens de Lange (1989) are relevant here. In a simulation exercise based on a social accounting matrix (SAM), he assessed the likely economic impact of various macroeconomic policies, including a publicly funded housing programme. His conclusions appear at first sight to be rather optimistic. An increase in housing expenditure of 1 per cent of GDP, financed by a deficit, is estimated to lead to an employment increase of 3,57 per cent, or some 250 000 formal sector jobs. However, the size of this effect has more to do with the multiplier characteristics of Roukens de Lange's SAM than the sectoral shifts which result from the housing programme. For instance, if the housing programme is funded by means of an increase in taxes, then the model predicts a 0,80 per cent increase in employment, representing only 60 000 employment opportunities. The multipliers used by Roukens de Lange may well be exaggerated. Contemporary macroeconomic theory suggests that one cannot give unqualified support to the basic Keynesian multiplier model.

In any event, the question of the size of the multiplier is not directly relevant to the central issue in this chapter, which has to do with maximising the employment-intensity of output rather than the growth rate of output. Even if a large multiplier was associated with deficit-financed expenditure then it would be more appropriate to discuss it in the context of a growth strategy. An employment strategy is primarily concerned with ensuring that a given level of growth is employment-intensive. The input–output projections considered here suggest that the unique employment effects of housing programmes, as well as other components of inward industrialisation policies, are not likely to add substantially to employment creation *per se*. The problem is that although the first-round effects of, say, a housing programme are labour-intensive, the second and higher-order backward linkages involve fairly capital-intensive sectors of the economy. Of course, if these policies succeed in providing a 'kick-start' to the economy, then they are to be highly recommended as growth strategies. In addition, it is also important to stress that many interventions associated with inward industrialisation, such as its housing and urbanisation components, are important in their own right, and are justifiable without reference to their potential employment spin-offs.

The World Bank's (1990) poverty report comes out in favour of more export-oriented growth strategies. It argues that industrial protection reduces the use of labour in the formal sector and that 'as a rule, the greater the degree of protection, the greater the capital intensity of production' (World Bank, 1990, p. 61). A more neutral trade regime would therefore tend to promote a more labour-utilising pattern of growth, in respect both of export- and import-competing sectors. Again, it is not certain that South Africa fits this model exactly. It has been firmly established that import-substitution industrialisation has been one of the causes of the rise in the capital intensity of manufacturing, and that a switch towards an export-orientation is consistent with the objective of creating more employment opportunities (Holden and Holden, 1981). Moreover, the economy clearly needs to export successfully if it is to attain a reasonably rapid rate of output growth.

But what is less certain is whether South Africa's export performance can be built on the basis of labour-intensive manufacturing industries. There is a strong body of opinion which points to the changing nature of the international division of labour and the need to be competitive in terms of information and capital-intensive goods. However this issue might be resolved, the fact of the matter is that most of South Africa's main manufactured exports, such as base metals, chemicals, paper, and even food, are relatively capital-intensive. The reason for this is that the comparative advantage of South Africa's manufacturing lies in the processing of primary goods. While some of the more labour-intensive sectors, such as wood, leather, furniture and clothing, increased their shares of total manufacturing exports between 1965 and 1985, they are all still comparatively minor exporters, with a combined share of 2,4 per cent of total manufactured exports (Standish and Gallaway, 1991). In addition, there are also some capital-intensive industries (base metals and paper) which managed to expand their export shares. The future pattern of export performance will presumably be similarly mixed, comprising some successful labour-intensive sectors, as well as some fast-growing capital-intensive ones.

To conclude, the argument developed in this section points to the uncertainties which surround the interactions between employment promotion and general growth strategies. Whatever the merits of the various growth options, it does not appear that any particular strategy is likely to bring unique and major advantages to the employment-creating process.

Factor markets

In the discussion on the nature of unemployment it was argued that factor price distortions, while not necessarily the major cause of rising unemployment, have certainly made a contribution. The problem is that the cost of capital may be artificially low, while wages may exceed their market-clearing levels. Policies to address distortions to the cost of capital are easy to identify since the problem arises largely as a result of government intervention. The present government has, in fact, already begun to implement the necessary adjustments. It has, for instance, undertaken to ensure that real interest rates are positive in future. The government is also trying to work towards a more neutral tax environment.

Suitable wage policies are much more difficult to prescribe. In the first place, wages are not particularly amenable to government manipulation, except in the context of a general incomes policy. But even if it were possible to intervene more actively, there is still a question about the desirability of attempting to control wages. The source of the deviation of wages from their market-clearing level is critical. For instance, if firms are paying efficiency wages, a cut in wages may be accompanied by a decline in productivity and growth, with little impact on unemployment. On the other hand, it is possible to find efficiency wage models in which cooperative responses to wage disequilibrium can have a major impact on unemployment (Summers, 1988). The point is really that wages may enter the economy in more complex ways than simple demand and supply curves suggest. One of the unfortunate consequences of this increased complexity is that a coherent set of wage policy prescriptions can no longer be derived.

The appropriate wage policy in the context of an unemployment problem that may have been aggravated by union or insider wage pressure is also controversial. The conservative response is to attempt to reduce the extent of the monopoly power enjoyed by insiders, whether organised or unorganised. This may take several forms and include, say, measures to constrain the scope of union prerogatives and activities. Such direct attacks are, however, unworkable and, for obvious political reasons, undesirable in South Africa. Exposing the economy to more internal and foreign competition, and providing for easier entry conditions, on the other hand, will not merely limit the monopoly power of insiders, but ought to be accompanied by productivity gains, thus allowing employed workers to preserve their wages. The potential conflict between the wage claims of the employed and the job prospects of the unemployed may thus be resolved constructively by means of the market. The growth of the informal sector should be viewed in this light.

In the final analysis, whether these strategies are implementable depends on the macroeconomic stance adopted by the union movement. It is now fairly well established that the structure of the bargaining process has a major influence on unemployment and its interaction with wages. It has recently been claimed that the relationship between the bargaining system and employment is hump-shaped (Calmfors and Driffill, 1988; Freeman, 1988). Decentralised systems, it is argued, facilitate labour market competition and a large degree of wage flexibility. This is one of the reasons why Japan, Switzerland and the US have relatively low unemployment rates. Corporatist or centralised systems of bargaining, such as those found in Austria and the Nordic countries, encourage the parties in the bargaining process to recognise broader interests, and to set wages which take account of their consequences for unemployment. Again, their unemployment rates are low. Intermediate systems, where bargaining occurs at the industry level, might be the most susceptible to unemployment and labour-market rigidities since the interests of the unemployed are not articulated within any of the bargaining forums.

The implications for policy of the above evidence, which appears to be surprisingly robust, are not clear. But it does seem as if South Africa's industry-based bargaining institutions are sub-optimal. The exportability of labour-market institutions is, however, a difficult issue. As Freeman (1988) notes, centralised labour markets might be workable only in smaller economies. The intensity of industrial conflict in South Africa could be another obstacle to a corporatist solution. Much more work on the subject clearly needs to be done. For the moment it must suffice to note that there is at present an opportunity for innovative change to the functioning of South Africa's labour market. Such possibilities are not likely to present themselves again.

Labour market policies

Labour market policies are a form of supply-side intervention. They can be justified if there is a possibility that unemployment may be reduced through measures which promote a more effective matching of unemployed workers and vacancies. Examples of labour market policies are job search services, training facilities and public works programmes. The first-mentioned include various measures aimed at assisting the unemployed to search for work. Designed to improve information flows in the economy, they reduce frictional aspects of unemployment. Training which is targeted at the unemployed will have similar effects, although in this instance the intention is to reduce the time it takes for the labour market to adjust to structural change and to eliminate a possible mismatch between the demand and supply of skills. A training programme of this sort has been one of the cornerstones of Swedish employment policy since the 1930s.

The considerable dispersion of unemployment rates among OECD countries has provided an opportunity for economists to analyse the effects of alternative labour market policies and institutions on the level and persistence of unemployment. In recent years expenditure on such policies has risen quite sharply. Although conditions in South Africa are very different, some of the results seem to be relevant.

One of the more comprehensive evaluations of labour market interventions concluded that countries with active labour market policies recover more rapidly from recessions. Moreover, unemployment persistence seems to be negatively related to such interventions (Jackman et al., 1990). Examples of countries which spend above-average amounts on labour market policies include Germany, Belgium, New Zealand and the Nordic economies. The idea that these policies are effective has, however, not gone unchallenged. Calmfors and Nymoen (1990), in an analysis of employment policies in the Nordic countries, argue that it is precisely the shift away from such measures that explains part of the low unemployment performance of these economies in recent years. The evidence they cite is, however, based on a single regression of wage flexibility against the level of participation in labour market programmes. The balance of the evidence is still in favour of active labour market programmes.

Loots (1989), in his version of inward industrialisation, argues that similar labour market policies should be introduced in South Africa. His proposal is to combine rapid urbanisation with special recruitment and training mechanisms, meant to enable new arrivals from the rural areas to adapt more rapidly to the urban economy, whether in the formal or informal sector. Several of the frictional problems of the South African labour market are thus addressed simultaneously. Although the immediate impact of these measures might be confined to the informal sector, there is no doubt that judicious intervention along these lines would facilitate labour absorption once the economy starts to grow again. Rapid urbanisation may be particularly relevant since it would permit much greater participation by women in the economy.

South Africa's unemployed also need more extensive training opportunities. Such programmes have of course been tried before. The special employment programme of 1985/86 set aside R50 million for the training of unemployed workers. It appears that there was a strong desire to participate in the project as it was consistently oversubscribed. By the end of the fiscal year some 160 000 people had been trained or were entering some process of training. Furthermore, of the first 40 000 who had completed a course, 25 per cent were placed in jobs via the programme itself. A similar, and possibly more extensive, project of this form ought to be considered seriously. Again, most of the benefits will accrue only if the formal sector begins to expand. At the same time, it is possible that appropriate training could open up more opportunities for self-employment, especially if it promotes the incorporation of blacks into activities which have been the preserve of whites until now.

Sector-based policies

It has been one of the central tenets of this chapter that it would be unwise to allow the need for employment creation to influence the choice of growth strategy significantly. Irrespective, however, of which general growth strategy is adopted, there is some scope for implementing policies directed at facilitating greater utilisation of labour within particular sectors of the economy. The most obvious sectors to consider are the agricultural, informal and public sectors.

From the earlier discussion it is apparent that the informal sector has become a fairly substantial employer of between 15 and 25 per cent of the workforce. The recent informal sector survey of the Central Statistical Services (*Statistically Unrecorded Economic Activities*) also shows that the incomes generated by the sector amount to 7,3 per cent of GDP. This is not an insignificant figure. To put it in perspective, the contribution of agriculture to GDP has for some time been below 6 per cent. The role of informal activities in relation to poverty relief is even more significant. Van der Berg (1990) estimates that the informal sector raises black per capita income levels by no less than 50 per cent. The widespread perception that informal work generates such meagre incomes that there is little point in encouraging it is therefore incorrect. The CSS survey arrived at an estimate for the average income earned in the sector of R534 per month (1989), with a median of about R300 per month. The average of R534 does not compare too unfavourably with an average wage of R958 per month for Africans in the manufacturing sector, and is more than four times the cash and in-kind remuneration received by Africans in agriculture.

Table 7.6.   Distribution of informal sector incomes in 1989

Monthly Income (R)	Percentages
0–150	32,3
150–350	28,3
350–600	17,3
600–1000	9,0
1000 +	13,1

Source: Statistically Unrecorded Economic Activities (1990).

Informal sector incomes are of course relatively unequally distributed, as is illustrated in Table 7.6. Many of the members of the sector earn modest incomes. In interpreting this table, it is worth bearing in mind, however, that the majority of the participants in the sector work on a part-time basis.

The champions of the informal sector have largely been drawn from the ranks of the free-marketeers. Proponents of this perspective have tended to make exaggerated claims on behalf of the sector, and may even have used these to justify a non-interventionist stance towards the unemployment problem. The left, on the other hand, has viewed the sector with a degree of suspicion. This is partly a consequence of ideological reservations about the market-orientation exemplified by informal work. But this opposition is also an effect of the potential for competition between the informal sector and more organised workers in the formal sector.

Both of the above positions are inappropriate. The informal sector is evidently not a complete solution to the unemployment problem. One has to be sensitive to the difficulties which the sector encounters in its interaction with the formal sector. Nattrass (1990), for instance, points to the possibility for destructive competition with the formal sector. But the neglect of the sector on the part of the left is equally untenable. The evidence cited above shows that the sector has to play a major role in any employment-creation and anti-poverty programme. It is really the only sector of the economy that showed any sustained growth during the 1980s. There can also be little doubt that there is room for further growth, especially in small-scale manufacturing. The marginal returns to appropriate interventions such as deregulation, although of a more determined kind than has been seen until now, can still be significant. Other support measures, such as access to subsidised credit and improved infrastructure, should also be upgraded (Ncube and Sisulu, 1991).

There are also some opportunities to promote labour absorption within the public sector. Ligthelm and Kritzinger-Van Niekerk (1990) provide some suggestions along these lines. They argue that government departments should in all cases carefully consider whether a particular project can be executed by using more labour-intensive production processes. They even moot the possibility of introducing certain norms as a guide to government planning. There may also be some room for introducing a bias towards labour when it comes to procurement practices. Finally, Ligthelm and Kritzinger-Van Niekerk argue that a switch in government spending towards poorer communities and an expansion in urban and rural development projects would automatically have a beneficial impact on employment.

These suggestions deserve to be pursued vigorously, especially in view of the enormous size of the public sector. It is, however, difficult to estimate the magnitude of their employment effects. Even marginal adjustments to employment norms in the public sector could have major effects on employment. On the other hand, there are some obvious limitations to these interventions. For example, a greater emphasis on black education will not have significant net employment benefits since the cost of labour in education is fairly high. There are also obstacles in the way of using more labour-intensive methods in public projects. The cooperation of the union movement, in particular, will be necessary in order to achieve a switch in the employment-orientation of the public sector in urban areas.

Another form of public sector intervention that has to be considered is a public works programme (PWP). In a related discussion of welfare policy Nattrass and Roux (in this volume) propose the introduction of a special employment programme for South Africa. The motivation behind the proposal is to provide desperately poor households with some relief by enabling them to find work at low wages. The emphasis is therefore on fighting extreme cases of poverty. The employment component is meant to act primarily as a mechanism for selecting the recipients of welfare transfers. This type of welfare programme should, however, be distinguished from a more conventional public works programme. The latter usually focusses on providing jobs that pay almost as well as the formal sector.

A conventional public works programme cannot be recommended uncritically. It is popularly assumed that any jobs created by a PWP represent net additions to the aggregate pool of employment opportunities. This is, of course, not necessarily the case. The conventional argument is based on an incorrect partial equilibrium analysis. Within a general equilibrium perspective it is obvious that the introduction of a PWP implies a redirection of resources from certain usages towards others. The jobs which are created must, therefore, be accompanied by some offsetting job reductions elsewhere in the economy.

The exact shape of this tradeoff is open to dispute. At one extreme is the traditional Keynesian position, in which PWPs are viewed as instruments of demand management. Under conditions of recession and under-utilisation of resources a PWP can lead to a general expansion via the multiplier process, and may even end up by creating more jobs than those immediately associated with the PWP. At the other extreme we find the general equilibrium market-clearing interpretation of the economy. In terms of this approach it is not possible to have market failure resulting in unutilised resources.

In between these poles a number of other positions exist. The two polar positions certainly have fewer adherents nowadays than in the past. The simplistic Keynesian view is probably no longer sustainable, particularly in the context of long-run unemployment. On the other hand, the incorporation of market failure within neoclassical general equilibrium models is almost standard practice today. Whatever the case may be, it is unlikely that theory can resolve this question. Interpretations of unemployment vary substantially, and influence one's understanding of the general equilibrium properties of an economy. For example, if unemployment is primarily of an efficiency-wage type, then a PWP will not necessarily contribute towards solving the problem. These circumstances may be contrasted with unemployment arising from a mismatch between the supply and demand for skilled labour. In these cases a well-targeted PWP may well have significant effects.

The uncertainties, both with regard to the nature of unemployment in South Africa and to the likely general equilibrium effects of a PWP, make it advisable to be cautious about introducing a full-scale public works programme. The same reservations do not, however, apply to a welfare-oriented employment project, which would be aimed at redistributing small amounts of income towards the very poor rather than at creating meaningful jobs. Furthermore, to caution against a conventional PWP does not imply opposition to attempts to encourage the public sector to use more labour-intensive techniques generally.

CONCLUSION

The only real solution to the unemployment problem is to be found in economic growth. The poor performance of the economy is ultimately responsible for the inability of the formal sector to absorb sufficient quantities of labour. One of the more controversial conclusions of this chapter is that none of the alternative growth strategies that were under consideration by the major actors in the economic policy debate in 1990, was clearly superior in terms of its employment-creation prospects. It is uncertain whether either inward industrialisation or export-led growth would generate a particularly labour-absorbing pattern of growth.

There is room for a variety of other policies to promote greater labour absorption. The evidence suggests that an artificial lowering of the cost of capital has caused excessive capital deepening throughout the economy. Efforts to remove the relevant factor price distortions on the capital side should continue. It is, however, more difficult to make unambiguous recommendations about wages, as the process of wage determination is rather complex. Although there are numerous theoretical models of wage inflexibility, it is not always clear what recommendations flow from these, or whether they are applicable to South Africa. The dilemma is clearly illustrated with regard to the trade unions. They are undoubtedly responsible for an element of wage inflexibility, but it is not certain whether this is very significant. In any event, it is even more difficult to specify an unambiguous policy response to the monopolistic power of trade unions. One thing is sure, an attempt to attack them directly is not desirable. It will be more appropriate to search for a social contract that makes due allowance for the interaction between wages and unemployment.

Policies directed at specific sectors of the economy are important. The role of the labour-intensive informal sector is emphasised above. Recent evidence shows that it is a vital stop-gap in the fight against unemployment and poverty, while its rapid growth during the 1980s suggests that the returns to further support for this sector will be high. It should therefore be promoted vigorously. Establishing norms to encourage labour-intensive methods in the public sector also deserves attention. As the public sector is large, even marginal adjustments can have a noticeable impact on unemployment. Labour market policies aimed at bringing about a more effective match between workers and jobs should also be considered. Training opportunities for the unemployed along the lines of those offered by the 1985/86 special employment programme may be useful, especially since they may promote greater labour absorption when the economy starts to grow again.

8

Conclusion:
What redistributes and what doesn't

PETER G. MOLL

Redistribution is one of the most important items on the South African political agenda. Since apartheid entailed a redistribution from blacks to whites, there is a widespread expectation that the death of apartheid must result in a redistribution from the rich to the poor, which would entail considerable redistribution from whites to blacks. The moral force of the demand for redistribution is overwhelming. Apartheid confiscated resources from blacks and directed them to serve the needs of the minority white population. So blacks – and here I include coloured people and Asian people – have bases for redress. It is unacceptable that South Africa be the country with the most unequal distribution of income in the world and be characterised by widespread grinding poverty, as the monumental work of Wilson and Ramphele (1989) has shown. Of economically active people in South Africa, 28 per cent of white males had tertiary qualifications, while fewer than 1 per cent of African males had them in 1985 (Archer and Moll, forthcoming). A string of shocking statistics could be supplied, but the point is clear that no future government or political party – or economist! – can afford to ignore the call for redistribution.

This concluding chapter pulls the findings of the earlier chapters together and in so doing presents the case for feasible redistribution. My chain of reasoning proceeds as follows. I first ask: *Who are the poor?* For without identifying the target of the intended redistribution wasteful mistakes can be made which end up giving substantial resources to, say, the middle classes. I then ask: *What are the constraints?* For without knowing, at least roughly, the limits of the state's redistributive capacities, wildly optimistic strategies might be chosen whose unintended consequences thrust the economy into contraction, inducing political tensions that often bring right-wing military dictatorships to power. Then, with the intended recipients and the constraints in mind, I ask: *What redistributive instruments work?* In the South African case, the results give great cause for hope – hope not for an American middle-class way of life for all in five years, but at least hope for significant improvement in the long term. I proceed to ask: *What instruments don't work?* There are a few particularly dangerous strategies that should be avoided at all costs. They become their own gravediggers, failing to redistribute either because they do not reach the poor or because they ignore the constraints. Finally, I ask: *Is this perspective politically feasible?* For however good it looks in a learned economics journal, if the whole concept is politically unpalatable, the whole exercise is futile and utopian and we economists will have to return to the drawing-board.

WHO ARE THE POOR?

The words 'the poor', 'the masses', 'the people' are frequently used by commentators and activists on the right, the left and the centre of the political spectrum. From an economist's point of view their meaning is often wide of the mark. The public mind has an urban bias. People imagine that the poor of our society are the urban working class. To be sure, urban workers *are* poor by comparison with the middle class or with the people of the advanced industrial world. They are far from being the poorest in our society. The poorest people are to be found in rural areas, especially in the so-called homelands; they are typically people of very low skill and educational levels doing menial tasks such as casual agricultural work; and more often they are women and children than men.

In addition to the urban bias in the public mind, there is also a bias towards the articulate and well-organised. The better-educated workers in big firms in the urban areas, often aided by well-organised unions, are better able to articulate their grievances and pressurise for their redress than poorly educated, frequently unemployed workers, especially when these are located in rural areas.

Calculations of annual wages of African workers 1990 reveal a good deal.[1] In manufacturing, the annual wage was approximately R12 000, in mining R9 200. In the informal sector, operators made profits of about R4 800 per year, while the employees of these informal sector operators received about R2 700 annually. Labourers on white farms earned some R2 400. Worst off in the group of fairly regular income-earners were rural dwellers in the homelands, who made, very roughly, R1 400, including both wages and the value of their subsistence output. But we must go even lower than that! These income figures reflect the wages of people in employment of some kind. There are many who are not so fortunate. We do not know the exact number of the unemployed since the statistics collected by Central Statistical Services in Pretoria are of low quality. Estimates of 20 per cent to 40 per cent of the urban workforce are not uncommon, although there are important regional differences with the Eastern Cape, for instance, having a higher unemployment rate than the PWV region.

Another way of describing the poor is those with very few skills. South Africa's parlous education system is surely one of the most important generators of poverty. According to the 1985 census, in the age group of 15 to 24 years, 46 per cent of black (African) males and 43 per cent of females had not completed primary school. This is to be contrasted with China in 1982 (21 and 49 per cent), Colombia in 1973 (19 and 21 per cent), and South Korea in 1980 (18 and 34 per cent). As far as education is concerned, it appears that blacks (Africans) in South Africa are only a little better off than Zambians, of whom, in 1980, 47 per cent of males and 58 per cent of females had not completed primary school.[2] Again, it should be stressed that these people with few marketable skills are disproportionately located in rural areas.

If the organised urban working class was the poorest in our society, the policy consequences would be simple. We should simply try to increase the total remuneration of this group by redistributing income to it from the middle and upper classes. This could easily be done through industrial minimum wages and through greatly strengthening union bargaining power by legislative means if need be.

The policy requirements are totally altered if the organised urban working class is not the poorest. For the interests of this class and the interests of the disparate poorest groups identified above are not identical. In some ways their interests are actually opposed. For example, imposing very high minimum wages could result in a decrease in employment, which would be felt most acutely by potential new entrants to the labour force. This is not to criticise the unions. They have a right and a duty to protect the interests of their members. The point is rather that society has to look beyond the interests of the organised urban working class to consider those who are far worse off, if redistribution is to be effective.

What do the very poor – as identified above – need? Obviously both the short and the long term are important. There are many people, particularly children in rural and small-town areas, who need immediate relief because they are starving. In the medium term, there are people whose employment is so uncertain and whose wages are so low that they are simply unable to provide adequately even for their children's minimum education needs or for their families' health needs. They need access to free or low-cost education and health services. These needs must also be balanced against the need in the long term for families to be able to provide for themselves in terms of nutrition, shelter and so on. To do this there has to be a massive expansion of jobs which pay sufficiently and which last. While this list of needs is obviously far from complete, it does at least contain most of the very basic items. It is proposed that a policy of redistribution should aim in the first place to meet these needs without putting any of the poor in a worse situation than they were before. But if we are not to put at risk the welfare of any of the poor, then several constraints on policy appear immediately.

WHAT ARE THE CONSTRAINTS?

Perhaps the most severe constraint on redistributive moves by the government is *capital mobility*. South Africa is a small economy and is open with respect to trade. Capital can move quickly in and out in response to expected returns. This was seen dramatically when capital flowed out after Sharpe-ville, after Soweto in 1976 and after the 'Rubicon' speech in 1985. Macro-economic instability – balance of payments problems, reschedulings with the IMF, very high inflation – would instantly be met by capital flight. Similarly, sudden redistributive moves such as nationalisation or threats of nationalisa-tion would also induce a vast outward movement of investible funds. Even if exchange controls were tightened, they are ineffectual in the long run because any company engaged in overseas trade can underinvoice its exports and overinvoice its imports and deposit the difference overseas.

Further constraints arise from the state of the *international economy*. Growth rates are expected by most observers to continue at the low rates experienced in the 1980s. So other things being equal, South Africa's exports, which presently account for one-third of the total economy, are likely to grow at low rates. A related factor is the extraordinary export performance of the Pacific Rim countries, which enforces a costly tradeoff between wage levels on the one hand and South Africa's international competitiveness on the other.

Another constraint is the *sluggish South African economy*. Growth rates were low during the 1980s. The growth of gross domestic product, after taking account of inflation, was 2,0 per cent between 1979 and 1989, and during the latter half of the period, from 1984 to 1989, was only 1,5 per cent.[3] One of the reasons for this poor performance is that South Africa was perceived to be a risky investment environment. Business confidence, as of 1991, was low because future political developments were uncertain. Poten-tial investors faced two major uncertainties: (a) Will macroeonomic policies in the 'new South Africa' drive inflation through the roof, pushing the economy into recession and new business ventures into bankruptcy? Or will macroeconomic balance be maintained? (b) Will the new government em-bark on a series of nationalisations, or will it seek to achieve redistribution by other means? For whether or not nationalisation is achieved by confisca-tion or purchase, the original investors would have preferred to invest in a more secure environment, for example in the Far East, Botswana, Chile, or certain Eastern European countries.

Population growth exercises another powerful constraint. The South Af-rican population is growing at 2,5 per cent or more. Consequently, each year at least 800 000 youth enter the labour market, or would do so were opportunities available. But the growth of employment in the formal sector was a mere 0,6 per cent annually between 1980 and 1988. Consequently the country simply cannot afford policies that discourage employers from em-ploying people. Also, it implies that growth-reducing policies would carry high costs in terms of unemployment. This limits the government's scope for redistribution: risky 'big push' policies which could put the economy in a tailspin would carry high costs in terms of unemployment and are best avoided.

The overall tax rate constrains the total government budget. In South

Africa taxes are already some 30 per cent of GDP, above the tax rate for most less-developed countries. In some European and Scandinavian countries the overall tax rate is higher than this, but during the 1980s most of them underwent far-reaching tax reforms because it was felt that the tax structures, and the overall tax rate, were negatively influencing their growth performance. South Africa may already be near the point where additional taxes could harm growth performance. Now it must be accepted as inevitable (as Loots and Van der Berg have argued in this book) that the overall tax rate must eventually rise as the country develops. In several countries of Europe, government spending rose when the franchise was extended to the mass of the populace. The problem is that if the overall tax rate rises too far and too fast the effects on investment incentives would be serious. Loots suggests that the overall tax rate be increased by only 0,5 percentage points or at most one percentage point of GDP, and that only in years when there is positive GDP growth.

Another limitation is that on *social spending*. It should be borne in mind that South Africa's spending on health, education and welfare, which was approximately 10 per cent of GDP in the late 1980s, was a little *higher* than had been achieved by most of the now developed countries when they were at levels of per capita income comparable to those of South Africa today. The UK reached a level of per capita income equivalent to that of South Africa at present in about 1890, and was at that time spending about 2 per cent of GDP on health, education and welfare. The UK achieved a 10 per cent social spending level only after the Second World War. Sweden reached South Africa's level of per capita income in about 1915, but achieved a 10 per cent social spending level only in the 1950s.[4] The injustice is not so much that South Africa does not spend enough on health, education and welfare as that the distribution of spending is racially discriminatory and regionally very uneven.

Further, as Van der Berg's chapter in this volume points out, South Africa's social expenditure levels are not greatly out of line with other countries at comparable levels of development. Indeed, South Africa's educational expenditure of 5,6 per cent of gross domestic product (GDP) compares well with the average for middle-income countries (2,9 per cent), and is close to the highest in the developing world (6,4 per cent, in oil-rich Oman). Obviously the fact that the developing world's heaviest education spender stops at 6,4 per cent does not prevent South Africa from doing better. I do not subscribe to the conservative maxim that nothing should be done for the first time. However, there is something to be learned from these numbers. It would probably be unwise to raise social spending levels and consequently overall taxation to heights that are very far out of line with what was observed in the present developed countries in the last century and with what can be observed in other developing countries today.

In short: growth rates are not going to be high, so that growth of the government budget is limited; tax recoveries can be increased only by relatively small amounts; the urban workforce is expanding at rates that threaten serious disequalisation of incomes in the future; social spending cannot be expanded very much beyond current totals; and dramatic redistributive moves such as nationalisation or massive debt-financed spending increases are ultimately self-defeating because they drive out investment and employment. Putting together these constraints almost gives the impression that the state is hamstrung and that poverty and redistribution cannot be addressed seriously. This superficial impression is, fortunately, quite mistaken. The major thrust of the previous chapters is that there are many redistributive instruments available.

WHAT REDISTRIBUTIVE INSTRUMENTS WORK?

It is not the intention of this book to provide a set of concrete plans or blueprints for the new South African economy. There is not the space in the extent of a small volume like this to deal with every aspect of redistribution. In any case the political process has not yet moved far enough towards consensus as to how the economy should be structured to justify the compilation of detailed plans. The focus is rather on broad principles and on the methods of ensuring consistency among plans, and above all on the criteria for selecting programmes in such a way that the combination of all of these does not have adverse unintended consequences. In this section specific cases are presented and proposals are made, relating to health, education, employment, and other issues. They are intended to provide examples and guidelines which, as the research develops and unfolds, will need to be replicated in every sphere of the economy.

Terence Moll has provided us, in his two chapters, with one of the most comprehensive reviews of the mechanisms of redistribution available anywhere in the development literature. Although there are significant inter-country differences, it is clear that we in South Africa have much to learn from the scores of experiments in redistribution which have been attempted in other developing countries in the past few decades. We also hear of some repeated mistakes which unhinged entire redistributive programmes.

One of the central points emerging from the study of other developing countries is that redistribution can work in a sustained and long-term manner only in the context of a growing economy. Indeed it is widely accepted by most of the anti-apartheid organisations that economic growth is an essential component of a redistributive strategy. In turn, rapid growth can be achieved only within a framework of macroeconomic balance, which means keeping the government budget deficit within manageable proportions and controlling the rate of inflation. Some of the conditions under which this can be achieved are outlined by Brian Kahn in his chapter in this volume. International experience indicates that when the foundations of economic growth and macroeconomic balance are present, a combination of a number of judiciously selected instruments can significantly enhance the quality of life of the very poor.

As Lieb Loots stresses in his chapter, it is virtually impossible to redistribute through the tax system alone because the vast majority of people in less-developed countries like South Africa pay very little tax anyway. Therefore giving them tax relief and taxing the rich more heavily does not *on its own* redistribute income. So the concern should be twofold: (1) to make the tax system as efficient a collector of revenue as possible, and then to spend the monies by targeting the poor accurately; and (2) to restructure the tax system so that it facilitates economic development and growth.

For the tax system to collect revenues efficiently it must be seen to be acceptable by the majority of the population. The impression that the working classes are given at the moment is that their incomes are taxed by income taxes and GST or VAT, while capital gains and wealth are barely taxed at all. In order to restore the credibility of the tax system, there must be an element of perceived redress. Justice must be done and be *seen* to be done. To satisfy this broader concept of efficiency – viz political efficacy – a restructuring of the tax system is unavoidable.

Hence it seems appropriate to introduce three forms of wealth taxation which have not been stressed in the past: a land tax, a property tax, and a capital transfer tax. Because of the large size of the base, the tax rates imposed would not have to be high, nor would this be desirable from the point of view of efficiency. Furthermore, a minimum tax could be placed on companies, using revenue or some other such measure as a base, in order to counteract the tendency of many firms to make accounting losses year after year by exploiting complexities in the tax law, and to ensure that efficient companies are rewarded. Again, the rate imposed should be low as the intention here is to aim at efficiency and not revenue collection. A similar proposal is to eliminate tax expenditures and incentives; there are so many of these that the tax system becomes overloaded and none has the desired output effects. In the aggregate, then, much the same amount of tax would be collected each year, the shifts in the tax system tending to cancel one another out.

The important question then becomes: how best to spend the available monies? Van der Berg in this volume provides us with some valuable estimates both of the 'savings' to be made from eliminating apartheid and of the costs involved in arriving at inter-racial parity in government spending. It is welcome to know, from his work, that some 3 or 4 per cent of GDP is available as 'free money' from the reduction of military spending and the elimination of apartheid. That *something* would become available is scarcely new. What is new is the quantification he provides. It is surprising, at first glance, how little cash is freed. Given all the immense pain inflicted by apartheid on so many people, it seems well-nigh incredible that the death of apartheid leaves a legacy of a mere 1 per cent or at the most 2 per cent of GDP. Together with another 2 per cent of GDP shorn from the military's share of 4 per cent in 1990, and with 0,4 per cent[5] from eliminating the shocking waste of the government's still-born decentralisation efforts, it seems we can count on getting about 3,4 per cent of GDP in 'free money'.

Now contrast these paltry 'savings' with the scale of legitimate needs. According to one estimate, racial equalisation of social spending at the levels received by white beneficiaries in 1990 would increase this category from the 1986 level of 9,5 per cent of GDP to some 30,8 per cent. The 'savings' that Van der Berg unearthed would cover at most one-sixth of the increase needed! So we would have to look into the possibility of increasing the size of the budget by heavier taxation. But the tax rates required to achieve this would induce a scale of capital flight far exceeding that brought about by sanctions.

Alternatively, the budget could be extended by borrowing. But as several of the chapters in this volume have shown, high levels of borrowing bring their own dangers. It is futile to attempt to be over-precise about the limits here, but to give some idea of the magnitudes, South Africa's budget deficit (as conventionally defined) was very roughly 3 per cent of GDP in 1990, and data from other developing countries suggest that a deficit of 7 per cent over a period of time eventually issues in very high inflation or in embarrassing reschedulings with the International Monetary Fund. The Fund's rule of thumb is that the deficit should be kept to 2–4 per cent. Combining the 'savings' of 3,4 per cent of GDP, a tax increase of 1 per cent of GDP, and an increase of the budget deficit of, say, 2 per cent of GDP (i.e. an increase from 3 per cent to 5 percent), we are still left with only an extra 6,4 per cent of GDP, whereas we would like to have 30,8 – 9,5 = 21,3 per cent of GDP.

However crude this number-juggling, it supplies an unambiguous conclusion: racial equalisation at current white levels is impossible at the present time given South Africa's level of economic development. Racial equalisation will have to be achieved at substantially lower levels of expenditure per capita.

Nattrass and Roux, in their chapter on welfare spending, go a step further and argue that racial equalisation is not enough. The present structure of spending is not accurately targeted on the poor. Terence Moll's survey of developing countries showed that this phenomenon is by no means uncommon: in many countries the middle class is the beneficiary of government largesse. Hence one should enquire whether there is a case for radical redistribution *within* each vote, in addition to racial equalisation. To go into the details of how to do this in the vast fields of education, trade, social pensions, housing, etc., would be impossible in the space of a short book. A great deal more research and data collection is needed in all these areas. Nattrass and Roux accordingly focus on three specific aspects: primary health care, nutritional interventions, and special employment programmes.

They show that dramatic improvements in the quality of life of the very poor can be achieved at surprisingly low cost by redirecting expenditures appropriately. International evidence suggests that high-impact primary health care services can be provided at a cost of $5 or less per capita per year. Rough calculations suggest that South Africa's entire population could be provided with such services at a cost less than one-tenth of the R7,4 billion allocated to health spending in 1989/90. Even if these international estimates are on the low side, the point is clear that there is tremendous scope for moving away from subsidisation of expensive capital-intensive health care for better-off urbanites towards widely spread basic services for everyone.

Broomberg (1991) calculates that a subsidy of approximately R160m was given to users of private hospitals in 1989. The implicit subsidy arose from the deductibility of medical payments from taxable income. It is quite unnecessary for the state to provide subsidies of this magnitude for people in the income bracket which requires them to use private hospitals. A radical restructuring of the health services of South Africa is called for.

Special employment programmes are designed to provide employment at modest wage levels to all who apply. They can be fairly well targeted by implementing them on a regional basis, and particularly in rural areas where both seasonal and long-term unemployment are common. Again, it would appear that there is considerable scope for using special employment programmes in South Africa to provide a social security net for the very poor. One rough estimate is that half a million people could be employed in such an arrangement at a cost below 1 per cent of GDP.

Although this volume does not pretend to address thoroughly the question of education spending, some ideas can briefly be supplied as to how to implement the principles of feasible redistribution in this area. It has been shown that if the government spent the same amount on *all* children – including those in the homelands, on farms owned by whites, and those not in school at all – as it spent in 1988/9 on every white child, the total cost would be R37 billion (in 1988/9 rands), which amounts to 18 per cent of GDP. Education spending in 1990 comprised some 5–6 per cent of GDP. The heaviest education spender in the developed world was Belgium, at 8 per cent of GDP, and the heaviest in the developing world was Oman, at 6,4 per cent. It is extremely unlikely that the funds would be forthcoming to expand education spending in South Africa to some three times its present level, so as to ensure racial equalisation at current white levels.[6]

What about equalisation at a lower level – say the coloured level? It has been shown that if the coloured per capita spending level were extended to all groups, whites and Asians would lose, but Africans would gain, and the total cost would be some R20 billion, in 1988/9 rands, amounting to some 10 per cent of GDP. Even this is very high, entailing almost a doubling of current education spending as a proportion of GDP. It is not beyond the bounds of possibility that South Africa could become the heaviest education investor, topping even Belgium and Oman. However, it is unlikely that education would be given so large a share of the budget, since there are urgent demands arising from every vote for any increase in the government's total outlay. But even with this very heavy spending we achieve only the coloured spending level.[7]

And so we are forced to delve further, and radically redistribute within the education vote so as to ensure that the poor get onto the first rungs of the employment ladder. This might be done by concentrating, say, 60 per cent of all education spending on universal and free primary schooling, 30 per cent on secondary schooling, and 10 per cent on tertiary education. This would – in time, because more teachers would have to be trained – enable all South Africa's children to gain access to primary schooling of reasonable quality, perhaps even a quality superior to that in the coloured system as of 1990. As the economy grows, it would become possible to extend the number of places in the secondary school system, but in the meantime rationing would have to be applied. This might be done by, for instance, having full state subsidisation of secondary schools only in certain regions – rural areas, townships, etc. – and requiring schools in the presently white suburbs to charge fees.

At the tertiary level, subsidies would not go to universities as they do at present. They would be directed to students in the form of loans and grants, awarded on the basis of need as determined by the tax returns of the student's parents. The middle classes, established and aspirant, would not be impressed as university fees would rise considerably, and some of the universities would no doubt convert themselves into more market-oriented institutions such as technikons. From the distributional point of view, however, this arrangement would be optimal because intelligent students from very indigent backgrounds would at last have access to the finest universities.

Another area which merits careful examination but which will not be discussed in detail here is land reform. As Terence Moll has shown in his review, land reform has often succeeded in redistributing resources of land, capital and skills to the poor, and it can also increase employment levels. Since the important question of land reform has been addressed in several other current works[8] I shall mention no further detail here, except for one forgotten element: agricultural taxation.

A study of agricultural taxation in Namibia (P. Moll, 1991b) revealed that the tax breaks available to farmers and not available to non-farm businesses far exceeded in value the direct subsidies which the farming sector received. The Namibian agricultural tax system is similar to that of South Africa. It was shown that if the agricultural tax concessions were abolished, the total tax paid by the large-scale commercial farming sector would rise more than fourfold. The most prominent concessions were (a) the 'standard value' method of valuing livestock for tax purposes, (b) the averaging of tax rates over five-year periods, and (c) full deductibility of development and improvement expenses from taxable income.

South African commercial farmers also enjoy these three concessions. Much research needs to be done to establish their value, but back-of-the-envelope calculations suggest that more than R100 million would be forthcoming in extra taxes annually if they were withdrawn. These funds could be directed towards land reform. The concessions should be removed for equity reasons because there is no reason why farmers should have privileges that miners, traders and manufacturers do not. They should also be removed for efficiency reasons, because the concessions draw resources out of productive non-agricultural uses into commercial farming, rendering the sector bigger than the market would have made it unaided, and driving up land prices.

The unemployment issue is one of the most serious redistributional questions. In South Africa, as in most countries, the labour market is by far the biggest of the factor markets – more than double the size of the shares, land and property markets. Although labour earnings are distributed more equally than returns from shares, land and property, the sheer size of the labour market ensures that most inequality is generated by the disparity of labour earnings, i.e. wages and salaries. In turn, widespread open unemployment is one of the big generators of inequality in the labour market. By implication, the expansion of employment would help reduce inequality and poverty.

The solutions to the unemployment problem may be divided into three areas: economic growth, wage policy, and labour market policies. First, regarding economic growth, during the 1980s the expansion of GDP was very slow, and this served to slow the growth rate of employment to a point well below the growth rate of the labour force. Political instability and uncertainty, together with slow international economic growth, and the effects of sanctions, combined to depress investment incentives and greatly reduce the amount of investment capital entering the country. Widespread open unemployment will probably persist until such time as the growth rate of the economy picks up, and this is largely a political question. Potential investors, local and foreign, do not take into account only the rate of profit that they might earn in year one. They are concerned about long-term returns and wish to know that their investments will not be wasted by a damaging hyperinflation, or through a huge increase in tax rates, or through a forced sale. Thus, for instance, the fighting between Inkatha and the ANC depresses business confidence, and apart from the appalling cost in lives, is also damaging to employment.

Similarly the enthusiasm for nationalisation in some of the liberation movements helps to create an atmosphere of uncertainty in which business leaders are unlikely to invest productively and increase employment rates. A leaf might be taken from SWAPO's book. The Namibian government avoided self-defeating national pride by giving guarantees to local and foreign investors that there would be no nationalisation, and made provision for investors to sue the government in terms of international law in foreign courts in case of any irregularity. If the liberation movements were to offer similar guarantees they could improve South Africa's growth and employment performance during the transition and then inherit a more powerful economy when they come to power.

The second set of solutions to unemployment lies in the area of wage policy. In an environment of slow economic growth and high unemployment, one would expect real wage levels to fall. This is because queues would build up at factory gates and applications pile up in personnel offices, which would embolden management to try to secure their labour needs at lower levels of wages. Also, trade unionists would not push for big wage increases, for fear of unemployment. And if wage levels fall, it would become more attractive for managers to use labour rather than to use machines. So the economy possesses a built-in stabilising force which would eventually reduce unemployment, even in the context of a slow growth record. Poor growth performance would be reflected in lower wages rather than in open unemployment.

This did manifestly not happen in South Africa in the 1980s, as André Roux points out. Despite high and perhaps increasing levels of unemployment, and despite the country's poor growth performance, unskilled wage levels in the formal sector (after taking account of inflation) were more or less constant between 1980 and 1985. After 1985 there were reductions in wages but these were small, certainly not large enough to induce managers to expand employment significantly. In short, the labour market appears to have been characterised by 'downward wage inflexibility', to use the jargon.

The problem in selecting appropriate wage policy is that we have very little clarity as to the causes of wage inflexibility. Several culprits may be imagined, but none of these is very convincing, as André Roux shows. And in any case in the present environment in South Africa it is politically unacceptable to adopt a policy of wage reduction. The so-called informal sector does, however, provide something of a way out. By 'informal sector' is meant the sector that cannot easily be taxed or recorded – for example, small-scale trade, peddlers, and unregistered taxis. André Roux shows that the informal sector in South Africa represents about 15 to 25 per cent of the workforce and 7 per cent of GDP. It is larger than the large-scale agricultural sector which accounts for less than 6 per cent of GDP. The very existence of the informal sector probably counts as evidence that there are many people who would be willing to work at wages below the level of wages in the formal sector, but who cannot find jobs in it. Policies of deliberately fostering the informal sector through the provision of credit and infrastructure should be continued and extended in order to accommodate as many of these individuals as possible.

The third set of solutions to unemployment lies in the area of labour market interventions. Roux presents the case that centralised collective bargaining would be superior to the present industry- and firm-based structure of bargaining. This is because industry- and firm-based bargainers tend to be preoccupied solely with the wage and can afford to ignore outsiders – the unemployed. By contrast, the duty of the participants in centralised bargaining processes is to consider the interests of *all* workers, and unavoidably the interests of the unemployed have to be considered. In times of poor economic performance and high unemployment, this probably leads to greater moderation in wage demands and hence to higher employment levels than would be the case under South Africa's present semi-centralised arrangements. Several additional solutions should be mentioned briefly: the extension of state-funded training schemes; the maintenance of positive real interest rates;

and instituting a special employment programme, as mentioned above.

WHAT REDISTRIBUTIVE INSTRUMENTS DON'T WORK?

For brevity I shall deal with only two putative redistributivist instruments which have been seriously proposed in South Africa in recent years. These are what has been termed 'macroeconomic populism' and nationalisation with compensation.

Macroeconomic populism

Funds for redistribution can be obtained either by reallocating within the existing budget, or by increasing the tax level, or by government borrowing. It is frequently a temptation for new left-leaning governments to aim at swift rejuvenation of the economy through 'redistribution with growth'. The argument is that the unequal distribution of income hampers the growth of local markets for home goods. If the government can 'kick-start' the home market by massive redistribution, then growth will take off. For instance, the government might embark on a huge housing programme, a vast increase in education spending, an increase in welfare payments, or a minimum wage strategy. Even if heavy government borrowing is required, the latter programmes will, in the long haul, more than pay for themselves. It is also argued that since the consumption pattern of the poor is more labour-using and less import-intensive than that of the rich, redistribution of income can lift some of the constraints on growth.

In the South African version, macroeconomic populism has assumed the title 'growth through redistribution'. The focus is especially on housing, since housing needs have been neglected in the past and it is believed that housing has important linkages to the rest of the economy so that heavy government spending in this area, even if it increases the budget deficit, would rejuvenate the economy.

This view can be criticised. First, one cannot always assume that the economy is in a Keynesian-type situation, in which there has been a temporary cutback in demand, so that all government needs to do is 'prime the pump' to get the economy back to full employment, without fear of inflation. Careful investigation would be needed to establish whether there are in fact significant unused resources available. Otherwise the injection of government finance might run up against bottlenecks, driving up prices, and in the long term could add significantly to the inflation rate.

This is not to say that spending on shelter is bad. Attention to the needs for shelter of the burgeoning urban population is urgently required. One way to address the problem is to divide the present housing budget up equally among all possible claimants, thereby providing capital subsidies which, housing experts tell us, would pay for a serviced site for *all* families in the urban areas. This would be a highly egalitarian way of redistributing the existing funds available for housing. As more budgetary resources become available, the strategy could shift to provide further money for the erection of structures. There is a danger in *starting* a massive programme building complete houses – viz that the money will run out after a time, leaving the chosen few in houses and the many with nothing at all, not even a serviced site.

So the criticism being made here is not against the desire to help people with accommodation. The criticism is levelled at the belief that a huge housing programme, financed by a government deficit if need be, would get the economy going again. We cannot be certain what would happen, but we would at least have to be aware that there might be sore disappointments in store if prices or interest rates or both rose instead and the economy continued to be sluggish.

Second, one cannot always assume that the consumption patterns of the poor are import-saving and labour-using. This is an empirical matter and needs to be examined carefully before this strategy is advocated as a major step in the direction of poverty reduction. Terence Moll has provided us with a thorough review of the developing-country literature in this regard, and it indicates that the import-saving and labour-using effects, when favourable, are most often not very strong. Even if the first-round effects are labour-using and import-saving, further work would have to be done to show that the second-round and subsequent effects would not reverse these beneficent effects.

Third, and perhaps most important, there are limits attaching to the size of the budget deficit, as Brian Kahn's chapter in this volume stresses. When the budget deficit becomes large, interest rates are driven up, which is unpopular with businesspeople and with house purchasers, so the government is tempted to 'monetise' the deficit, in other words to create money with which to pay for the goods and services being purchased. Eventually this can lead to high rates of inflation.

In sum: it is not impossible that a massive housing programme would have a favourable impact on the economy. However, there are several ways in which such a programme could be derailed, especially through an inflationary budget deficit. Much more careful investigation is required before a reasonable assurance could be given that the envisaged 'growth through redistribution' would succeed.

Nationalisation

During 1990 there occurred an important shift in the stance of the African National Congress regarding nationalisation of industry. Although its position had not always been unambiguously stated, it was generally understood that prior to 1990 the ANC favoured nationalisation without compensation. The statements of Murphy Morobe in this regard are well known, and the deputy president, Nelson Mandela, declared in January 1990, shortly before his release from prison, that the 'mines, banks and monopoly industry' would be nationalised, and that any departure from this policy was inconceivable. Later in the year, however, ANC spokesmen softened their stance. They now allowed for the possibility of compensation, even full compensation, and nationalisation would be undertaken only in specific cases after careful study had revealed that it would be in the interests of the people. The criteria by which the interests of the people would be judged were not made clear.

In this section I wish to show that a substantial nationalisation experiment, even if executed in this very moderate manner, is probably not a means of redistribution. I have no argument with nationalisation *per se* or with a small nationalisation experiment paid for in cash; the concern here is to demonstrate that if redistribution is the objective, a concerted effort at nationalisation, even nationalisation of this attenuated kind, is unlikely to achieve it.

The first objection to nationalisation with compensation is that it would probably have adverse effects on investment incentives. This may sound strange: if the shareholders are being *fully* compensated, why would they have any objection to being bought out? The point is that if there is a substantial nationalisation move it is most unlikely to be executed by means of up-front cash payments. The cash would simply not be available because the sums involved would be huge. More likely is that payment would take the form of a combination of cash and government bonds, with cash probably taking a minor role. The credibility of the government bonds would be in question. There have been so many cases in which new governments with redistributivist objectives have followed policies which result in very high inflation rates, that the expropriated shareholders and other investors would fear that the value of their government bonds would be greatly reduced by inflation.

Of course the government might not pursue an inflationary policy. But potential investors do not know this in advance. All they do know is that many other governments with redistributivist objectives have allowed inflation rates to soar. In short, they would become reluctant to invest, fearing that they might be expropriated and be given compensation which would include a government bond element whose value would be eroded by increasing inflation rates. So even the greatly moderated nationalisation position of the ANC as of late 1990 would tend to reduce economic growth rates, with damaging effects on wages and employment, which would, if anything, exacerbate the maldistribution of income.

The second reason why nationalisation (with compensation) would probably not turn out to be redistributivist is that the mechanisms whereby redistribution would be achieved have never been made clear. The motives for nationalisation are undefined. Is it the first step on the road to socialism? Is it a means of raising wages of workers in nationalised firms? Or providing them with security of employment? Will nationalisation be used to increase employment, at some sacrifice of profits? Is the objective to reduce monopoly or oligopoly powers and thereby engineer lower prices for consumers? Or is it a means of giving workers control over the factories?

The motives given for nationalisation thus far are irritatingly vague. Some of them are contradictory – for example, should the surplus be used to reduce output prices or to pay workers better? In any case, some of the purposes for which nationalisation might be used would not help the poorest at all. It is not widely appreciated that workers in large, 'nationalisable' firms, who are usually also better educated and more highly skilled and unionised, are mostly earning wages above the median. Nationalisation aimed at raising wages, financed through budget deficits or taxation, might redistribute from taxpayers to the above-median worker, but would not improve the quality of life of the poorest – the unemployed, the informal sector workers, rural people, etc. Until such time as the mechanism of redistribution is clearly specified, and all the other non-redistributivist motives for nationalisation are openly rejected, it would be naive to assume that nationalisation has a good chance of helping the poor.

IS THIS PERSPECTIVE POLITICALLY FEASIBLE?

The public might be forgiven if, after reading this book, they get the feeling that academic economists are an unfeeling bunch who are unmoved by the ringing calls for dramatic economic transformation: they are wet blankets when it comes to nationalisation, they constantly warn of constraints on budget deficits and taxation levels, and they even pooh-pooh middle-of-the-road strategies like growth through redistribution.

There is a huge gap in communication between academic economists on the one hand and the general public and the political parties on the other. So it is essential to ask: can the people of South Africa be convinced by the general approach being advocated here? Or are these redistributive instruments so utterly lacking in glamour that South Africa is fated to suffer a period of policy gyrations and consequent economic convulsions – so that after a decade the men in uniform intervene to restore order, leaving democracy and redistribution as the major casualties? The combination of measures proposed in this book can, with some confidence, be predicted to bring steady but gradual improvement in the long haul. There is little doubt in my mind that this vision is superior to the litany of poorly conceived promises of dramatic reparations, which would probably be followed by equally dramatic reversal. But can enough people be convinced?

It is clear that many people's expectations – such as they flared up during the political upheavals of the 1980s – cannot be met. The question is whether the political parties, or at least the most important among them, as well as the majority of their supporters, can be convinced that steady improvement over the long term is the maximum that can be achieved in almost any economy, certainly in the stressed South African one. The issue is whether the anxiety for swift redress can be channelled productively.

There are several factors which indicate to me that there is a fighting chance that a more cautious and gradualist approach to redistribution might eventually be adopted. First, the liberation movements, and in particular the ANC, have already demonstrated considerable flexibility by changing their stance on a number of key issues, such as nationalisation. It is possible that the leadership in these organisations would further moderate their positions as the time for the assumption of power comes closer.

Second, it is of major concern to every liberation movement that the economic policies it introduces in its first years of power do not undermine its chances of succeeding at the polls at the next election. Hence if a tolerably democratic system is brought about in South Africa it is quite possible that the ruling coalition will very seriously take into account the effects of its economic policies on economic growth and labour markets in the longer run. While it may well be necessary to use the lurid language of massive expropriation in the run-up to the election, there are many examples, Zimbabwe and Namibia being only two of the most recent, in which the policy stance after the election has been far more accommodating towards market processes.

The third reason for believing that South Africans may eventually choose a piecemeal approach to redistribution is that foreign institutions such as the World Bank, the International Monetary Fund, and other aid, research and advisory organisations are able to exercise considerable influence over domestic policy. I am not referring to the explicit conditionality that attaches to the granting of loans, but to the widespread and invisible effect on the attitudes and the understanding of policymakers, politicians, academics, bureaucrats and others that accompanies intensive contacts with the personnel and the procedures of these international institutions. A culture of economic policy thinking is communicated as conferences are held, papers are delivered, and visits and personal interchange are organised. Given that the international mood is growth-oriented, and that the local mood is redistribution-oriented, the melding of the two may result in redistribution that is effective in the long term.

Notes

---

1. Microeconomic redistributive strategies in developing countries

The author would like to thank the Leverhulme Trust for financial support, enabling him to reserch and write this and the following chapter.

(1) The approach parallels that of Ahluwalia and Chenery (1974a, p. 48).

(2) Issues of economic justice are not considered below. These are important, however, to the planning of any redistributional strategy: who should pay for and who should benefit from redistribution, and why?

(3) Collectivist land reforms will not be discussed here as their record is so consistently poor and political support for them in most developing countries appears to be lacking. One exception is the case of Chile between 1964 and 1973 (Foxley et al., 1979, pp. 218–231; Brown, 1989). Land reform appears to have worked in large part because the reform units created – termed asentamientos (settlements) – typically corresponded to the expropriated farms, less any reserve left to the former owner, and were viewed as temporary; in many areas, mixes of collective and family enterprises were eventually chosen, to preserve certain economies of scale while dividing up land devoted to field crops (Brown, 1989, p. 223, 237). In Zimbabwe, most white farms were subdivided into peasant plots, despite a government preference for producer cooperatives to take them over ('Model B') (Palmer, 1990, p. 168).

(4) Cline even suggests that in many cases, output should rise so much that "land reform with full compensation is financially feasible if implemented over time" (1977, p. 319).

(5) This constraint was encountered by land reforms in Chile after 1964; by about 1967, large unproductive farms had been dealt with and modern well-managed ones were an entirely different kettle of fish (Brown, 1989, p. 228). Similar issues were central in the Zimbabwean land-reform debates (Moyo, 1988).

(6) Many redistributional goals regarding large firms can be achieved in a range of ways, including partial state ownership, careful regulation, and so on. Some of the alternatives are discussed below.

(7) In the jargon, the price elasticity of labour demand. This is measured as the percentage by which labour demand increases in response to a one per cent decrease in the real wage.

(8) This skills constraint regarding states directing large firms is similar to that faced when nationalising them, except that the necessary skills are more easily learnt over time.

(9) Such programmes may, however, raise worker productivity and lower fertility rates and can thus provide economic benefits (Burki and Ul Haq, 1981).

(10) More formally, consumption spending can be regarded as having low social rates of return and investment spending as having high social rates of return, though these are usually unquantifiable.

(11) Many developing countries have suffered large government budget deficits owing to rising consumption subsidies (Tanzi, 1982, Table 7).

(12) A similar problem may be faced by Zimbabwe during the 1990s, as suggested by

numbers for school graduates given in Chung (1988).

(13) In many cases, redistributive strategies had social and political goals to do with national self-determination and the undermining of politically regressive classes (cf. Lowenthal, 1983). Such goals will not be discussed here.

(14) Though inheritance and other taxes, combined with wars and exogenous events, substantially reduced the long-run income shares of the richest property-owners in some developed countries.

2. Macroecomomic redistributive packages in developing countries

(1) This 'structuralist' explanation of sluggish economic growth is discussed by Sutton (1984) and T. Moll (1988).

(2) Williamson observes that populist economics can be simply defined: "redistribution not disciplined by a budget constraint" (1990, p. 3n4). Its political link is that populist economics is based on "policies designed to evoke consensus, for they are intended to work to the benefit of some but to the detriment of no one" (Ffrench-Davis, 1976, p. 110).

(3) Various price indexes are available for Chile in the early 1970s, often differing for reasons which are not explained (compare Sutton, 1984, Table 2.1; Sachs, 1989, p. 160; Dornbusch and Edwards, 1990, Table 1). Official indices underestimate inflation by recording prices at controlled levels when many goods were traded at black market prices or were unavailable. The numbers quoted in the text are mostly from Dornbusch and Edwards (1990, Table 1), and try to allow for this problem.

(4) This narrowing, however, was small; the often-quoted numbers for Taiwan, for example, suggesting a fall in the household Gini coefficient from 0,56 in 1953 to 0,31 in 1964 (Fei *et al.*, 1979, p. 35, 56), are statistically indefensible (T. Moll, 1990, pp. 12–13).

(5) The evidence on these issues is discussed by Fields (1985), Oshima (1990) and T. Moll (1990), who also deals with the experiences of Malaysia, Thailand, Indonesia and Costa Rica.

(6) It should be noted, however, that the East and Southeast Asian record suggests 'unskilled' workers need some education and skills to work efficiently, a minimum often being six to eight years of schooling (T. Moll, 1990, p. 3). Poor developing countries lacking abundant workers with basic education may have comparative advantages in producing only (certain) agricultural products and natural resources.

(7) This section does not deal with debates about how to characterise redistributive regimes and their bases of support, covered in Latin American cases by Ascher (1984, ch. 1), Dix (1985) and O'Donnell (1979).

(8) It should be noted, however, that Adelman, Morris and Robinson are dealing with a country with a rather equal income distribution to begin with, while the distributional shifts which they regard as small – a change of below 5 per cent in the Gini coefficient, or a change of below 20 per cent in a percentile's share of GDP (1976, p. 575) – might be viewed as fairly large by other observers, and could sometimes do a great deal to eliminate absolute poverty.

4. Deficit financing and redistribution in South Africa

(1) Capital expenditures include expenditures by departments on goods and services resulting in capital formation, or the establishment or acquisition by the state of fixed capital assets such as land, buildings and structures. Recurrent expenditure is expenditure on goods and services not intended for the establishment or acquisition of capital assets. The major recurrent expenditure is public service wages and salaries.

(2) Although the primary deficit focusses on current expenditure on goods and services, it is not clear that it is the only relevant measure for assessing the effect on crowding out. To the extent that debt issues do affect real interest rates, this will also have an effect on the decisions of the private sector to invest. In addition, an increasing proportion of interest payments in government expenditure could affect the long-run sustainability of budget deficits.

(3) These funds include various government pension funds, social security funds and the Guardian's Fund.

(4) Some countries' Central Bank Acts (e.g. Botswana) put direct limits on the amounts of new security issues that the Central Bank can take up. Although the original Reserve Bank

legislation (the Currency and Banking Act, No. 31 of 1920) placed severe restrictions on the Reserve Bank as a source of credit to the government, these restrictions were eased in 1941 (and retained in the 1944 Reserve Bank Act). The Act allowed the Reserve Bank to invest in government securities up to a total amount equal to its paid-up capital and reserve fund plus one-third of its liabilities to the public.

5. Redirecting goverment expenditure

(1) Note that housing was for present purposes excluded. Parity in education, health and social pensions would not have implied exactly equal per capita expenditure, given differences in age structure and social pension eligibility of the different groups.

(2) Calculations based on Benso, 1982, Table 64; *South African Statistics 1988*, p. 7.26; and *South African Labour Statistics 1989*, pp. 105 and 351.

(3) Personal communication, Department of Transport.

(4) Reduced state debt cost was to be effected by 'prudent budgeting, lower inflation rates and lower interest rates'.

6. Making welfare spending work

(1) Pensions are the main examples of these in South Africa (see, e.g., Le Roux, 1990). It is at this stage unlikely that other forms of social security on a significant scale will be introduced in the short term.

(2) The World Bank provides some figures to back its claim that low proportions of spending on health are associated with poor performance of quality of life indicators and vice versa (1990, p. 46). However, this conclusion seems to be more a function of the selection of countries presented than a statistical rule which is capable of standing up to a wider sample.

(3) The observations in this and the preceding paragraph were formed in discussion with Max Price at the Wits Medical School and Di McIntyre at the UCT Medical School.

(4) Estimates which he took into account included (a) vaccine doses against measles, diphtheria, pertussis, polio, BCG and tetanus at $1,20 a child in 1985 (this includes an estimate for transport and wastage); (b) per capita costs of 15 essential drugs (including transport) to village health posts of 50–60c a year in 1985; and (c) sachets of oral rehydration salts at 60–80c per child per year. Estimates for the provision of primary health care services varied across countries, depending on the scale of services provided and the cost concept used (ibid., p. 171).

(5) We are grateful to Ken Andrew for providing us with his background workings for the illustrative budget.

(6) An interesting experiment is currently taking place in Zimbabwe where communities are being offered employment guarantee schemes at the cost of cuts in state spending in areas such as health and education. This gives communities a greater say in how they raise and reallocate revenue. It is a more participatory, decentralised variant of redistributing from richer members of the community to poorer members.

7. Options for employment creation

(1) In the jargon this responsiveness is called the output elasticity of employment. It is measured as the percentage increase in employment in response to a 1 per cent increase in output.

8. Conclusion: What redistributes and what doesn't

(1) Calculations from P. Moll (1991c), Chapter 5.

(2) All these educational statistics from Archer and Moll (forthcoming). The original sources are the authors' calculations from the 1985 South African Census microdata, and the most recent published censuses for the other countries.

(3) *Statistical/Economic Review in Connection with the Budget Speech 1990/91*. Pretoria: Government Printer, page 6.

(4) Data in this paragraph from P. Moll (1991c), Chapter 2.

(5) Decentralisation cost R826 million in 1989, and GDP was some R237 001 million (*Statistical/Economic Review 1990/91*).

(6) Data in this paragraph from P. Moll (1991c), Chapter 7.

(7) Data in this paragraph from P. Moll (1991c), Chapter 7.

(8) E.g. De Klerk (1991); and P. Moll (1991c), Chapter 8.

References

Abedian, I. and B. Standish, 1984. An analysis of the sources of growth in state expenditure in South Africa 1920–1982. *South African Journal of Economics* 52.

Abedian, I. and B. Standish, 1986. Public works programme in South Africa. *Development Southern Africa* 3.

Abedian, I. and B. Standish, 1989. *Job Creation and Economic Development in South Africa*. Report prepared for the HSRC, Pretoria.

Adelman, Irma, 1988. A poverty-focused approach to development policy. In: Wilber, Charles K. (ed.). *The Political Economy of Development and Underdevelopment*. New York: Random House.

Adelman, Irma, Cynthia Taft Morris and Sherman Robinson, 1976. Policies for equitable growth. *World Development* 4.

Aharoni, Yair, 1977. *Markets, Planning and Development. The Private and Public Sectors in Economic Development*. Cambridge, Mass.: Ballinger.

Ahluwalia, Montek S. and Hollis Chenery, 1974a. The economic framework. In: Chenery *et al.* (1974).

Ahluwalia, Montek S. and Hollis Chenery, 1974b. A model of distribution and growth. In: Chenery *et al.* (1974).

Ahluwalia, Montek S., 1990. Policies for poverty alleviation. *Asian Development Review* 8.

Alam, M. Shahid, 1989. The South Korean 'miracle': examining the mix of government and markets. *Journal of Developing Areas* 23.

Allal, M. and E. Chuta, 1982. *Cottage Industries and Handicrafts. Some Guidelines for Employment Promotion*. Geneva, ILO.

Amsden, Alice H., 1990. Third World industrialisation: 'Global Fordism' or a new model? *New Left Review* 182.

ANC, 1990. Discussion document on economic policy. Johannesburg: African National Congress.

Archer, Sean, and Peter G. Moll, forthcoming. Education and growth in the South African economy: selected policy issues for discussion. In: Iraj Abedian and Barry Standish, forthcoming. *Economic Growth in South Africa: Selected Issues*. Cape Town: Oxford University Press.

Arida, Persio, 1986. Macroeconomic issues for Latin America. *Journal of Development Economics* 22.

Ascher, William, 1984. *Scheming for the Poor. The Politics of Redistribution in Latin America*. Cambridge, Mass. and London: Harvard University Press.

Balassa, Bela, 1988. Essays in Development Strategy. Occasional Paper No. 5, International Center for Economic Growth, Panama.

Ballentine, J. Gregory and Ronald Soligo, 1978. Consumption and earnings patterns and income distribution. *Economic Development and Cultural Change* 26.

Barker, F., 1986. South Africa's Special Employment Programme of R600 million. *Devel-*

opment Southern Africa 3.

Bean, C.R., P.R. Layard and S.J. Nickell, 1986. The rise in unemployment: a multi-country study. *Economica* 53 (Supplement).

Benso, 1982. *Statistical Review of Black Development 1982.* Vol.II: *The independent states.* Benso: Pretoria.

Bequele, Assefa and David H. Freedman, 1979. Employment and basic needs: an overview. *International Labour Review* 118.

Berg, A., 1987. *Malnutrition: What Can be Done? Lessons from World Bank Experience.* Baltimore: Johns Hopkins University Press.

Bergsman, Joel, 1979. Growth and equity in semi-industrialised countries. World Bank Staff Working Paper No. 351, Washington.

Berry, Albert and William R. Cline, 1979. *Agrarian Structure and Production in Developing Countries.* Baltimore: Johns Hopkins.

Biersteker, Thomas J., 1987. *Multinationals, the State, and Control of the Nigerian Economy.* Princeton: Princeton University Press.

Biggs, F.P., 1981. Aspects of combining capital and labour in South Africa. *Studies in Economics and Econometrics* 13.

Bird, R.M., 1987. A new look at indirect taxation in developing countries. *World Development* 15.

Blanchard, O.J. and L.H. Summers, 1988. Beyond the natural rate hypothesis. *American Economic Review* 78.

Blejer, M. and K.Y. Chu, 1990. Fiscal policy, labour markets, and the poor. Paper presented at the Third Annual Inter-American Seminar on Economics, Public Sector and Labour Markets in Latin America, Rio de Janeiro, 16–17 March 1990.

Boyd, Derick A.C., 1988. *Economic Management, Income Distribution, and Poverty in Jamaica.* New York: Praeger.

Bromley, Ray (ed.), 1985. *Planning for Small Enterprises in Third World Cities.* Oxford: Pergamon.

Broomberg, Jonathan, 1991. Private hospitals: are they good or bad for SA's health? *Business Day* (11 February).

Brown, Marion R., 1989. Radical reformism in Chile: 1964–1973. In: Thiesenhusen (ed.)

Brown Commission, 1986. *Enquiry into Health Services.* 6th Interim Report, RP 62/1986.

Browne, G.W.G., 1983. Fifty years of public finance. *South African Journal of Economics* 51.

Browne, G.W.G., 1984. Begrotingsbeleid. In Franzsen, D.G. (ed.), 1984. *Owerheidsfinansies in Suid-Afrika.* Butterworth: Pretoria/Durban.

Budget Review 1990. Republic of South Africa. Pretoria: Government Printer.

Burki, Shahid Javed and Mahbub Ul Haq, 1981. Meeting basic needs: an overview. *World Development* 9.

Calitz, E., 1986. *Aspekte van die vraagstuk van staatsbestedings-prioriteite met spesiale verwysing na die Republiek van Suid-Afrika: 'n Funksioneel-ekonomiese studie.* Unpublished D.Comm. thesis. Stellenbosch: University of Stellenbosch.

Calitz, E., 1989. Towards appropriate fiscal policy in South Africa. Paper delivered to the Colloquium on The Future South African Economy. Lausanne. 8–13 July.

Calitz, E., 1990. The potential of the South African economy to create sufficient job opportunities. Paper presented at the Biennial Conference of the Development Society of Southern Africa, 5–7 September.

Calmfors, L. and J. Driffill, 1988. Bargaining structure, corporatism and macroeconomic performance. *Economic Policy.*

Calmfors, L. and R. Nymoen, 1990. Nordic unemployment. *Economic Policy.*

Cauas, Jorge and Marcelo Selowsky, 1977. Potential distributional effects of nationalisation policies: the economic aspects. In: Frank and Webb (eds.).

Chenery, Hollis, Montek S. Ahluwalia, C.L.G. Bell, John H. Duloy and Richard Jolly, 1974. *Redistribution with Growth.* New York: Oxford University Press.

Chung, Fay, 1988. Education: revolution or reform? In: Stoneman, Colin (ed.). *Zimbabwe's*

Prospects. Issues of Race, Class, State and Capital in Southern Africa. London and Basingstoke: Macmillan.

Cline, William R., 1972. *Potential Effects of Income Redistribution on Economic Growth. Latin American Cases.* New York: Praeger.

Cline, William R., 1975. Distribution and development. A survey of literature. *Journal of Development Economics* 1.

Cline, William R., 1977. Policy instruments for rural income distribution. In: Frank and Webb (eds.).

Colman, David and Frederick Nixson, 1986. *Economics of Change in Less Developed Countries* (second edition). Oxford: Philip Allan.

Cook, Paul and Colin Kirkpatrick, 1988. Privatisation in less developed countries: an overview. In: Cook and Kirkpatrick (eds.).

Cook, Paul and Colin Kirkpatrick (eds.), 1988. *Privatisation in Less Developed Countries.* Brighton: Wheatsheaf.

Cornia, Giovanni Andrea, 1984. A summary and interpretation of the evidence. *World Development* (Special Issue: The Impact of the World Recession on Children) 12.

Cornia, Giovanni Andrea, 1985. Farm size, land yields, and the agricultural production function. *World Development* 13.

Cornia, G., 1987a. Economic decline and human welfare in the first half of the 1980s. In: Cornia, G., R. Jolly, and F. Stewart (eds.). *Adjustment with a Human Face: Protecting the Vulnerable and Promoting Growth.* Oxford: Clarendon Press.

Cornia, G., 1987b. Social policy making: restructuring, targeting, and efficiency. In: Cornia, G., Jolly, R. and F. Stewart (eds.) *Adjustment with a Human Face: Protecting the Vulnerable and Promoting Growth.* Oxford: Clarendon Press.

Cornia, G., 1989. Investing in human resources: health, nutrition and development for the 1990s. *Journal of Development Planning* 19.

Cornia, G., R. Jolly, and Stewart, F., 1987. An overview of the alternative approach. In: Cornia, G., Jolly, R. and F. Stewart (eds.) *Adjustment with a Human Face: Protecting the Vulnerable and Promoting Growth.* Oxford: Clarendon Press.

Cornia, Giovanni Andrea and Frances Stewart, 1990. The fiscal system, adjustment and the poor. Working Paper No. 29, Centro Studi Luca d'Agliano, Torino, and International Development Centre, Queen Elizabeth House, Oxford. Also: Development Studies Working Paper 29. Oxford: Queen Elizabeth House.

Croeser, G.P., 1990. A government view on the requirements for growth and development towards equality. Paper presented at the Joint German–South African Dialogue, 12 December.

Cukierman, A., 1987. Comment in Modigliani (1987).

Davies, Rob and David Sanders, 1988. Adjustment policies and the welfare of children: Zimbabwe, 1980–1985. In: Cornia, Giovanni Andrea, Richard Jolly and Frances Stewart (eds.). *Adjustment with a Human Face,* Vol. II. *Country Case Studies.* Oxford: Clarendon.

De Janvry, Alain, 1981. *The Agrarian Question and Reformism in Latin America.* Baltimore and London: Johns Hopkins.

De Klerk, Mike (ed.), 1991. *A Harvest of Discontent: The Land Question in South Africa.* Cape Town: Institute for Democratic Alternatives in South Africa.

De Loor, J.H., 1984. Die ekonomie van owerheidsuitgawes in Suid-Afrika. In: Franzsen, D.G. (ed.), 1984. *Owerheidsfinansies in Suid-Afrika.* Butterworth: Pretoria/Durban.

De Vylder, Stefan, 1976. *Allende's Chile.* Cambridge: Cambridge University Press.

De Wulf, Luc, 1975. Fiscal incidence studies in developing countries: survey and critique. *International Monetary Fund Staff Papers* 22.

Democratic Party, 1990. *A social market economy: manifesto and economic proposals.* Addendum: Financial implications: Budgeting for prosperity and development. Policy Position Paper. Cape Town: Democratic Party.

Development Bank of Southern Africa, 1987. *SATBVC Statistical Abstracts 1987.* Halfway House: Development Bank.

Diaz-Alejandro, Carlos F., 1981. Southern Cone stabilisation plans, In: Cline, William R. and Sidney Weintraub (eds.). *Economic Stabilisation in Developing Countries.* Washington:

Brookings Institution.

Diaz-Alejandro, Carlos F., 1983. Open economy, closed polity? In: Tussie, Diana (ed.). *Latin America in the World Economy*. Aldershot, Hampshire: Gower.

Dix, Robert H., 1985. Populism: authoritarian and democratic. *Latin American Research Review* 20.

Donaldson, A., 1987. Public projects: a spanner in the works. *Indicator SA* 5.

Donaldson, A., 1990. Growth, congestion and efficiency: problems in the restructuring of social services. Paper delivered at the Cape Colloquium on Redistribution and Growth in a Post-Apartheid South Africa, November.

Dopfer, Kurt, 1979. *The New Political Economy of Development. Integrated Theory and Asian Experience*. London and Basingstoke: Macmillan.

Dornbusch, Rudiger and Sebastian Edwards, 1990. Macroeconomic populism. *Journal of Development Economics* 32.

Dornbusch, R. 1987. Comment in Lessard and Williamson (1987).

Dorner, Peter and William C. Thiesenhusen, 1990. Selected land reforms in East and Southeast Asia: their origins and impacts. *Asian-Pacific Economic Literature* 4.

Dorner, Peter, 1972. *Land Reform and Economic Development*. Harmondsworth, Middlesex: Penguin.

Dreyer, J.P. and S.S. Brand, 1986. 'n Sektorale beskouing van die Suid-Afrikaanse ekonomie in 'n veranderende omgewing. *South African Journal of Economics* 54.

Durevell, Dick, 1989. *Zimbabwe*. Macroeconomic study No. 6, Planning Secretariat, University of Gothenburg, Sweden.

Espinosa, Juan G. and Andrew S. Zimbalist, 1978. *Economic Democracy*. New York: Academic Press.

Falkena, H.B., L.J. Fourie, and W.J.Kok, (eds), 1986. *The Mechanics of the South African Financial System*. Johannesburg: Macmillan

Falkena, H.B., W.J. Kok, and J.H. Meijer, (eds), 1987. *The Dynamics of the South African Financial System*. Johannesburg: Macmillan

Fei, John C.H., Gustav Ranis and F.W.Y. Kuo, 1979. *Growth with Equity: The Taiwan Case*. New York: Oxford University Press.

Ffrench-Davis, Ricardo, 1976. Policy tools and objectives of redistribution. In: Foxley, Alejandro (ed.).

Fields, Gary S., 1980. *Poverty, Inequality, and Development*. Cambridge: Cambridge University Press.

Fields, Gary S., 1984. Employment, income distribution and economic growth in seven small open economies. *Economic Journal* 94.

Fields, Gary S., 1985. Industrialisation in Hong Kong, Korea, Singapore, and Taiwan. In: Walter Galenson (ed.). *Foreign Trade and Investment. Economic Development in the Newly Industrialising Asian Countries. Madison, University of Wisconsin Press*.

Fields, Gary S., 1988. Income distribution and economic growth. In: Ranis, Gustav and T. Paul Schultz (eds.). *The State of Development Economics. Progress and Perspectives*. Oxford: Basil Blackwell.

Fields, Gary S., 1989. A compendium of data on inequality and poverty for the developing world. Unpublished paper, Cornell University.

Figueroa, Adolfo, 1976. The impact of current reforms on income distribution in Peru. In: Foxley, Alejandro (ed.).

Fine, Ben, 1990. Scaling the commanding heights of public enterprise economics. *Cambridge Journal of Economics* 14.

Finsterbusch, Kurt and Warren A. Van Wicklin III, 1989. Beneficiary participation in development projects: empirical tests of popular theories. *Economic Development and Cultural Change* 37.

Fitzgerald, E.V.K., 1976. *The State and Economic Development: Peru Since 1968*. Cambridge: Cambridge University Press.

Fitzgerald, E.V.K., 1979. *The Political Economy of Peru 1956–78*. Cambridge: Cambridge University Press.

Foxley, Alejandro (ed.), 1976. *Income Distribution in Latin America*. Cambridge: Cambridge University Press.

Foxley, Alejandro, in collaboration with Eduardo Aninat and J.P. Arellano, 1979. *Redistributive Effects of Government Programmes. The Chilean Case*. Oxford *et al.*: Pergamon.

Foxley, Alejandro and Dagmar Raczynski, 1984. Vulnerable groups in recessionary situations: the case of children and the young in Chile. *World Development* 12.

Frank, Charles R. and Richard C. Webb, 1977. An overview of income distribution in less developed countries: policy alternatives and design. In: Frank and Webb (eds.).

Frank, Charles R. and Richard C. Webb (eds.), 1977. *Income Distribution and Growth in the Less-Developed Countries*. Washington, D.C.: Brookings Institution.

Freedman, D., 1990. Special employment programmes in developed and developing countries. *International Labour Review* 129.

Freeman, Richard B., 1982. The changing economic value of higher education in developed economies. Report to the OECD. Discussion Paper No. 974, Harvard Institute of Economic Research, Harvard University.

Freeman, Richard B., 1988. Labour markets. *Economic Policy*.

Gaude, J., 1986. Capital–labour substitution possibilities: a review of empirical evidence. In: Bhalla, A.S. (ed.). *Technology and Employment in Industry* (third edition). Geneva: ILO.

Ghose, Ajit Kumar, 1983. Agrarian reform in developing countries: issues of theory and problems of practice. In: Ghose (ed.). *Agrarian Reform in Contemporary Developing Countries*. London and Canberra: Croom Helm.

Glewwe, Paul, 1988. Economic liberalisation and income inequality: further evidence on the Sri Lankan experience. *Journal of Development Economics* 28.

Glyn, A. and Rowthorn, B., 1988. West European unemployment: corporatism and structural change. *American Economic Review* 78.

Green, Reginald Heribold, 1978. A guide to acquisition and initial operation: reflections from Tanzanian experience 1967–74. In: Faundez, Julio and Sol Picciotto (eds.). *The Nationalisation of Multinationals in Peripheral Economies*. London: Macmillan.

Griffin, Keith and Jeffrey James, 1979. Problems of transition to egalitarian development. *The Manchester School of Economic and Social Studies* 3.

Griffin, Keith and Jeffrey James, 1981. *The Transition to Egalitarian Development*. London and Basingstoke: Macmillan.

Griffin, Keith and John Knight, 1989. Human development: the case for renewed emphasis. *Journal of Development Planning* 19.

Griffith-Jones, Stephany, 1981. *The Role of Finance in the Transition to Socialism*. Totowa, NJ: Allanheld.

Hanson, J., 1984. Food and nutrition policy with relation to poverty: the child malnutrition problem in South Africa. Carnegie Conference on Poverty in South Africa, paper number 205. University of Cape Town.

Herschbach, Dennis, 1989. Training and the urban informal sector: some issues and approaches. In: Fluitman, Fred (ed.) *Training for Work in the Informal Sector*. Geneva: ILO.

Hirschman, Albert O., 1981. *Essays in Trespassing. Economics to Politics and Beyond*. Cambridge: Cambridge University Press.

Hojman, David E., 1989. Neoliberal economic policies and infant and child mortality: simulation analysis of a Chilean paradox. *World Development* 17.

Holden, M. and P. Holden, 1981. The employment effects of different trade regimes in South Africa. *South African Journal of Economics* 49.

International Labour Organisation, 1985. *Informal Sector in Africa*. Addis-Abiba: ILO-JASPA.

Irish Tax Commission, 1982. *First Report*. Dublin: Irish Government Printer.

Isenman, Paul, 1980. Basic needs: the case of Sri Lanka. *World Development* 8.

Jackman, R., C. Pissarides, and S. Savouri, 1990. Unemployment policies. *Economic Policy*.

Jackson, P.M. and A.J. Palmer, 1988. The economics of internal organisation: The efficiency of parastatals in LDCs. In: Cook and Kirkpatrick (eds.).

Jarvis, Lovell S., 1989. The unravelling of Chile's agrarian reform, 1973–1986. In: Thiesenhusen (ed.).

Jayawardena, Lal, 1974. Sri Lanka. In: Chenery *et al.* (1974).

Jones, Leroy P. and Edward S. Mason, 1982. Role of economic factors in determining the size and structure of the public enterprise sector in less developed countries with mixed economies. In: Jones (ed.). *Public Enterprise in Less Developed Countries: Multidisciplinary Perspectives.* Cambridge: Cambridge University Press.

Jones, Leroy P. and Il Sakong, 1980. *Government, Business and Entrepreneurship in Economic Development: The Korean Case.* Cambridge, Mass.: Harvard University Press.

Jones, Leroy P., 1985. Public enterprise for whom? Perverse distributional consequences of public operational decisions. *Economic Development and Cultural Change* 33.

Kahn, B., 1991. The crisis and South Africa's balance of payments. In S. Gelb (ed). *South Africa's Economic Crisis.* Cape Town: David Philip.

Kannappan, Subbiah, 1985. Urban employment and the labour market in developing countries. *Economic Development and Cultural Change* 33.

Killick, Tony and Simon Commander, 1988. State divestiture as a policy instrument in developing countries. *World Development* 16.

Kim, Yoo Bae, 1989. Evolution of the Korean employment structure and labor market adjustment. *Asian Economies* 79.

Kock, A.D. and J.H. Meijer, 1987. Reserve Bank accommodation. In Falkena *et al.* (1987).

Kohl, JÜrgen, 1985. *Staatsausgaben in Westeuropa: Analysen zur langfristige Entwicklung der öffentlichen Finanzen.* Campus Verlag: Frankfurt am Main.

Koo, Bohn-Young, 1981. Role of foreign direct investment in recent Korean economic growth. Korea Development Institute Working Paper 8104, Seoul.

Krueger, Anne O., 1984. Comparative advantage and development policy 20 years later, In: Syrquin, Moshe, Lance Taylor and Larry E. Westphal (eds.). *Economic Structure and Performance. Essays in Honor of Hollis B. Chenery.* Orlando: Academic Press.

Krueger, Anne O., 1988. The relationships between trade, employment, and development. In: Ranis, Gustav and T. Paul Schultz (eds.). *The State of Development Economics. Progress and Perspectives.* Oxford: Basil Blackwell.

Kuznets, Paul W., 1988. Employment absorption in South Korea: 1970–1980. *Philippine Review of Economics and Business* 25.

Lall, S., 1989. Human resources development and industrialisation, with special reference to sub-Saharan Africa. *Journal of Development Planning* 19.

Laraki, K., 1989. Ending food subsidies: nutritional, welfare and budgeting effects. *World Bank Economic Review* 3.

Leineweber, Norbert. 1988. *Das säkulare Wachstum der Staatsausgaben: Eine kritische Analyse.* Vandenhoeck and Ruprecht: Göttingen.

Lehmann, David, 1978. The political economy of Armageddon: Chile, 1970–1973. *Journal of Development Economics* 5.

Le Roux, F. and S.J. van der Walt, 1987. Public debt management. In Falkena *et al.* (1987).

Le Roux, P., 1990. Which way with pensions in a post-apartheid South Africa? Paper delivered at the Cape Colloquium, Somerset West, 1990.

Lessard, D.R. and J. Williamson, (eds), 1987. *Capital Flight and Third World Debt.* Institute for International Economics.

Levy, Brian, 1988. The state-owned enterprise as an entrepreneurial substitute in developing countries: the case of nitrogen fertilizer. *World Development* 16.

Ligthelm, A. and Kritzinger-Van Niekerk, L., 1990. Unemployment: the role of the public sector in increasing the labour absorption capacity of the South African economy. *Development Southern Africa* 7.

Lindbeck, A. and Snower, D.J., 1986. Wage setting, unemployment, and insider-outsider relations. *American Economic Review* 76.

Lindbeck, A. and Snower, D.J., 1988. Long-term unemployment and macroeconomic policy. *American Economic Review* 78.

Lindbeck, A. and Snower, D.J., 1989. Macroeconomic policy and insider power. *American Economic Review* 79.

Lombard. J.A., 1988. Economic growth, structural change and inward industrialisation. Paper presented at the Sixth NAFCOC Industrial Conference, 25 April.

Loots, L.J., 1989. Unemployment, the public sector and the market. Paper presented at the Lausanne Colloquium, 8–13 July.

Loots, L.J., 1991. Tax policy, redistribution and growth. Economic Policy Paper Series. Economic Policy Research Project, University of the Western Cape.

Lowenthal, Abraham F., 1983. The Peruvian experiment reconsidered. In: McClintock, Cynthia and Abraham F. Lowenthal (eds.).

Luedde-Neurath, Richard, 1984. State intervention and foreign direct investment in South Korea. *IDS Bulletin* 12.

Lund, F., 1989. Dilemmas in South African welfare: the impact of past and present welfare patterns on future policy choices. Mimeo. Centre for Social and Development Studies, University of Natal.

Lustig, Nora, 1980. Underconsumption in Latin American economic thought: some considerations. *Review of Radical Political Economics* 12.

McClintock, Cynthia and Abraham F. Lowenthal (eds.), 1983. *The Peruvian Experiment Reconsidered.* Princeton: Princeton University Press.

McClure, Charles A., 1975. Taxation and the urban poor in developing countries. World Bank Staff Working Paper No. 222, Washington.

McGrath, M., 1983. *The distribution of personal income in South Africa in selected years over the period 1945 to 1980.* Ph.D. thesis, University of Natal, Durban.

McIntyre, D., 1990. Public sector health care expenditure in South Africa: 1970–1990. Health Economics Unit Working Paper no. 1. University of Cape Town.

Mallon, Richard D., 1981. Performance evaluation and compensation of the social burdens of public enterprise in less developed countries. *Annals of Public and Co-operative Economy* 52.

Margo Commission Report, 1987. *Report of the Commission of Enquiry into the Tax Structure of the Republic of South Africa.* Pretoria: Government Printer.

Mason, Edward S., Mahn Je Kim, Dwight H. Perkins, Kwang Suk Kim and David C. Cole, 1980. *The Economic and Social Modernisation of the Republic of Korea.* Cambridge, Mass. and London: Harvard University Press.

Meijer, J.H., 1986. Monetary policy and the instruments of monetary policy. In Falkena *et al.* (1986).

Mesa-Lago, Carmelo, 1986. Cuba's centrally planned economy: An equity trade-off for growth, In: Hartlyn, Jonathan and Samuel A. Morley (eds.). *Latin American Political Economy. Financial Crisis and Political Change.* Boulder and London: Westview.

Michell, Tony, 1988. *From a Developing to a Newly Industrialised Country: The Republic of Korea, 1961–82.* ILO, Employment, Adjustment and Industrialisation Study No. 6: Geneva.

Millward, Robert, 1988. Measured sources of inefficiency in the performance of private and public enterprises in LDCs. In: Cook, Paul and Colin Kirkpatrick (eds.).

Modigliani, F., 1987. The economics of public debt. In Razin, A. and E. Sadka (eds.) *Economic Policy in Theory and Practice.* Basingstoke: Macmillan.

Mohammad, Sharif, 1981. Trade, growth and income redistribution: a case study of India. *Journal of Development Economics* 9.

Mohr, Philip and Rogers, Colin, 1987. *Macro-economics.* Lexicon Publishers: Johannesburg.

Moll, Peter G., 1990. Inter-industry wage differentials and efficiency wages in South Africa. Economics Department, Northwestern University, Evanston. Mimeograph.

Moll, Peter G., 1991a. The effects of union wages in South African manufacturing. Economics Department, Northwestern University, Evanston. Mimeograph.

Moll, Peter G., 1991b. Subsidization, taxation and viability of the commercial agricultural sector. Background paper for the National Conference on Land Reform and the Land Question, Windhoek. Mimeo.

Moll, Peter G., 1991c. *The Great Economic Debate.* Johannesburg: Skotaville.

Moll, Terence C., 1988. 'The limits of the possible': Macro-economic policy and income redistribution in Latin America and South Africa. In: Suckling, John and Landeg White (eds.).

After Apartheid. Renewal of the South African Economy. London: James Currey.

Moll, Terence C., 1989. Employment, growth and structural change in the apartheid economy. Paper presented at the Lausanne Colloquium, 8–13 July.

Moll, Terence, 1990. Income distribution in developing countries. Unpublished paper, Institute of Development Studies, University of Sussex, Brighton.

Moore, Mick, 1990. Economic liberalisation, growth and poverty: Sri Lanka in long run perspective. Discussion Paper No. 274, Institute of Development Studies, University of Sussex.

Moran, Theodore H., 1974. *Multinational Corporations and the Politics of Dependence. Copper in Chile.* Princeton: Princeton University Press.

Morawetz, David, 1977. Employment implications of industrialisation in developing countries: a survey. In: Royal Economic Society and Social Science Research Council. *Surveys of Applied Economics* 2. London and Basingstoke: Macmillan.

Morawetz, David, 1980. Economic lessons from some small socialist developing countries. *World Development* 8.

Mosely, W. and R. Jolly, 1987. Health policy and programme options: compensating for the negative effects of economic adjustment. In: Cornia, G., R. Jolly, and F. Stewart (eds.). *Adjustment with a Human Face: Protecting the Vulnerable and Promoting Growth.* Oxford: Clarendon Press.

Moyo, Nelson, 1988. The state, planning and labour: towards transforming the colonial labour process in Zimbabwe. *Journal of Development Studies* 24.

Muir, K.A., M.J. Blackie, B.H. Kinsey and M.L.A. de Swardt, 1982. The employment effects of 1980 price and wage policy on the Zimbabwe maize and tobacco industries. *African Affairs* 81.

Nafziger, E. Wayne, 1988. *Inequality in Africa.* Cambridge: Cambridge University Press.

National Productivity Institute, 1990. *Productivity Focus 1990.* Pretoria: NPI.

Nattrass, N., 1990. The small black enterprise sector – a brief note of caution. In: Nattrass, N. and Ardington, E. (eds.). *The Political Economy of South Africa.* Cape Town: Oxford University Press.

Ncube, P. and Sisulu, M., 1991. Redistribution through the informal sector and small scale industries in a post-apartheid South Africa – some considerations. Economic Policy Research Project, University of the Western Cape. Mimeograph.

O'Donnell, Guillermo, 1979. *Modernisation and Bureaucratic-Authoritarianism.* Berkeley: Institute of International Studies.

OECD, 1979. *The Taxation of Net Wealth, Capital Transfers and Capital Gains of Individuals.* Paris: OECD Report.

OECD, 1990a. *Recent Tax Reform in OECD Countries and Prospects for the Nineties.* Paris: OECD.

OECD, 1990b. *Tax Policy and Reform for Foreign Investment in Developing Countries.* Paris: OECD.

Oppenheim, Lois H., 1989. The Chilean road to socialism revisited. *Latin American Research Review* 24.

Oshima, Harry T., 1990. Employment generation: the long-term solution to poverty. *Asian Development Review* 8.

Owens, J., 1990. *Financing Public Expenditure: The Role of Tax Reform and Designing Tax System.* Paris: OECD.

Palmer, Robin, 1990. Land reform in Zimbabwe, 1980–1990. *African Affairs* 89.

Paukert, Felix, Jiri Skolka and Jef Maton, 1981. *Income Distribution, Structure of Economy and Employment. The Philippines, Iran, the Republic of Korea and Malaysia.* London: Croom Helm.

Pedraza-Bailey, Silvia, 1982. Allende's Chile: political economy and political socialisation. *Studies in Comparative International Development* 17.

Phelps-Brown, Henry, 1978. *The Inequality of Pay.* Oxford: Oxford University Press.

Pinstrup-Andersen, P., M. Jaramillo, and F. Stewart, 1987. The impact on government expenditure. In: Cornia, G., Jolly, R. and F. Stewart (eds.). *Adjustment with a Human Face: Protecting the Vulnerable and Promoting Growth.* Oxford: Clarendon Press.

Porteous, David, 1990. Heart attack? Bank nationalization in South Africa: implications and alternatives. Unpublished paper, Economics Department, Yale University, New Haven.

Prosterman, Roy L. and Jeffrey M. Riedinger, 1987. *Land Reform and Democratic Development*. Baltimore and London: Johns Hopkins.

Race Relations Survey, various years. South African Institute of Race Relations: Johannesburg.

Rajapatirana, Sarath, 1988. Foreign trade and economic development: Sri Lanka's experience. *World Development* 16.

Ramanadham, V.V., 1984. *The Nature of Public Enterprise*. London and Sydney: Croom Helm.

Rao, D.C., 1978. Economic growth and equity in the Republic of Korea. *World Development* 6.

Ravallion, Martin, 1990. Market responses to anti-hunger policies: effects on wages, prices and employment. In: Dreze, Jean and Amartya Sen (eds.). *The Political Economy of Hunger* 2, *Famine Prevention*. Oxford: Clarendon.

Recktenwald, Horst Claus, 1981. Finanzwirtschaft, öffentliche. In Alber, Willi (ed.) 1981. *Handwörterbuch der Wirtschafs-wissenschaft (HdWW)*, vol.3. Ungekürzte Studienausgabe. Gustav Fischer/J.C.B.Mohr/Vandenhoeck and Ruprecht: Stuttgart/Tübingen/Göttingen.

Rodgers, Gerry (ed.), 1989. *Urban Poverty and the Labour Market: Access to Jobs and Incomes in Asian and Latin American Cities*. Geneva: ILO.

Rodrigo, Chandra, 1988. Statutory minimum wage fixing in the tea industry of Sri Lanka: determinants, trends and impact, 1945–79. In: International Labour Office. *Assessing the Impact of Statutory Minimum Wages in Developing Countries: Four Country Studies*. Geneva: ILO.

Rothstein, Robert I., 1976. The political economy of redistribution and self-reliance. *World Development* 4.

Roukens de Lange, A., 1989. The impact of macroeconomic policies on the South African economy: an analysis based on a social accounting matrix. *Studies in Economics and Econometrics* 13.

Sachs, Jeffrey D., 1989. Social conflict and populist policies in Latin America. In: Brunetta, Renato and Carlo Dell'Aringa (eds.) *Labour Relations and Economic Performance*. Basingstoke: Macmillan.

SACOB, 1990. *Economic Options for South Africa*. Johannesburg: South African Chamber of Business.

Sandbrook, Richard, 1988. Patrimonialism and the failing of parastatals: Africa in comparative perspective. In: Cook and Kirkpatrick (eds.)

Sandri, Renato, 1976. Chile: analysis of an experiment and a defeat. *Science and Society* 40.

SATEP, 1988. Minimum wage fixing in Botswana: implications for employment and income distribution. In: International Labour Office. *Assessing the Impact of Statutory Minimum Wages in Developing Countries: Four Country Studies*. Geneva: ILO.

Schafer, Michael, 1983. Capturing the mineral multinationals: advantage or disadvantage? *International Organisation* 37.

Schatz, Sayre P., 1981. Assertive pragmatism and the multinational enterprise. *World Development* 9.

Seeber, A.V. and J.A. Döckel, 1978. The behaviour of government expenditure in South Africa. *South African Journal of Economics* 46.

Seers, Dudley, 1981. Preface to: Griffith-Jones, Stephany. *The Role of Finance in the Transition to Socialism*. Totowa, NJ: Allanheld.

Selowsky, Marcelo, 1981. Income distribution, basic needs and trade-offs with growth: the case of semi-industrialised Latin American countries. *World Development* 9.

Sen, Amartya, 1981. Public action and the quality of life in developing countries. *Oxford Bulletin of Economics and Statistics* 43.

Sen, Amartya, 1989. Food and freedom. *World Development* 17.

Sheahan, John, 1983. The economics of the Peruvian experiment in comparative perspective. In: McClintock, Cynthia and Abraham F. Lowenthal (eds.)

Sheahan, John, 1987. *Patterns of Development in Latin America. Poverty, Repression, and*

Economic Strategy. Princeton: Princeton University Press.

Shilazi, Z., 1989. Reforming tax systems. *Tax Notes*, January 9.

Shilazi, Z. and L. Squire, 1988. *Tax Policy in Sub-Saharan Africa*. Washington, D.C.: World Bank.

Simkins, Charles, 1990. *The Urban Foundation income distribution model*. Phase one. Urban Foundation: Johannesburg. September.

South African Labour Statistics, various years. Central Statistical Service, Republic of South Africa. Pretoria: Government Printer.

South African Statistics, various years. Central Statistical Service, Republic of South Africa. Pretoria: Government Printer.

Standish, B. and D. Gallaway, 1991. Exports, efficiency and capital in South African manufacturing. Forthcoming in *Studies in Economics and Econometrics*.

Starr, Gerald, 1982. *Minimum Wage Fixing. An International Review of Practices and Problems*. Geneva: ILO.

Statistical/Economic Review in Connection with the Budget Speech 1990/91. Republic of South Africa. Pretoria: Government Printer.

Statistically Unrecorded Economic Activities (1990). Statistical News Release PO315, October. Published by Central Statistical Services.

Stewart, Frances, 1983. Payments systems and Third World development: some conclusions. In: F. Stewart (ed.).

Stewart, Frances (ed.), 1983. *Work, Income and Inequality. Payments Systems in the Third World*. London and Basingstoke: Macmillan.

Stewart, Frances, 1985. *Planning to Meet Basic Needs*. London and Basingstoke: Macmillan.

Stewart, F., 1987a. Supporting productive employment among vulnerable groups. In: Cornia, G., R. Jolly, and F. Stewart (eds.). *Adjustment with a Human Face: Protecting the Vulnerable and Promoting Growth*. Oxford: Clarendon Press.

Stewart, F., 1987b. Alternative macropolicies, meso policies and vulnerable groups. In: Cornia, G., R. Jolly, and F. Stewart (eds.). *Adjustment with a Human Face: Protecting the Vulnerable and Promoting Growth*. Oxford: Clarendon Press.

Stoneman, Colin, 1989. The World Bank and the IMF in Zimbabwe. In: Campbell, Bonnie K. and John Loxley (eds.). *Structural Adjustment in Africa*. Houndmills, Basingstoke: Macmillan.

Summers, L.H., 1988. Relative wages, efficiency wages, and Keynesian unemployment. *American Economic Review* 78.

Sutton, Mary, 1984. Structuralism: The Latin American record and the new critique. In: Killick, Tony (ed.). *The IMF and Stabilisation: Developing Country Experiences*. London: Heinemann.

Tanzi, Vito, 1974. Redistributing income through the budget in Latin America. *Banco Nazionale del Lavoro Quarterly Review* 108.

Tanzi, Vito, 1982. Fiscal disequilibrium in developing countries. *World Development* 10.

Terreblanche, S.J., 1989. Die konstitusionele ontwikkeling in Suid-Afrika met spesiale aandag aan die staatsfinansiële implikasies. *Tydskrif vir Geesteswetenskappe* 29.

Thiesenhusen, William C., 1989. Conclusions: searching for agrarian reform in Latin America. In: Thiesenhusen (ed.)

Thiesenhusen, William C. (ed.), 1989. *Searching for Agrarian Reform in Latin America*. Boston: Unwin Hyman.

Tokman, Victor E., 1983. The influence of the urban informal sector on income inequality. In: F. Stewart (ed.).

Tokman, Victor E., 1988. Urban employment: research and policy in Latin America. *CEPAL Review* 34.

Van der Berg, Servaas, 1989. Meeting the aspirations of South Africa's poor through market and fiscal processes. Paper delivered to the Colloquium on the Future South African Economy, Lausanne, 8–13 July. Published (without footnotes) in *Monitor (Journal of the Human Rights Trust)*, April 1990.

Van der Berg, S., 1990. On measuring the informal sector. Paper presented at a Symposium on the Production and Use of Socio-economic Statistics, 4 May.

Van Ginneken, Wouter (ed.), 1988. *Trends in Employment and Labour Incomes. Case Studies on Developing Countries.* Geneva: ILO.

Viljoen, F., H. Mueller, J. Bloomfield, J. Smith and H. van Zyl, 1987. Evaluation of the South African Special Programme for Creating Employment. Research Report 8, Development Bank of Southern Africa, Halfway House, March.

Wade, Robert, 1990. *Governing the Market. Economic Theory and the Role of Government in East Asian Industrialisation.* Princeton: Princeton University Press.

Webb, Richard C., 1976. The distribution of income in Peru. In: Foxley (ed.).

Webb, Richard C., 1977. *Government Policy and the Distribution of Income in Peru, 1963–1973.* Cambridge, Mass. and London: Harvard University Press.

Weeks, John, 1983. The state and income redistribution in Peru, 1968–76, with special reference to manufacturing. In: F. Stewart (ed.).

Weiner, Dan, 1989. Agricultural restructuring in Zimbabwe and South Africa. *Development and Change* 20.

Wells, J.R., 1977. The diffusion of durables in Brazil and its implications for recent controversies concerning Brazilian development. *Cambridge Journal of Economics* 1.

Whittaker, J., 1987. Monetary policy: its scope and limitations. *Social Dynamics* 13.

Whittaker, J and A.H. Theunissen, 1987. Why does the Reserve Bank set the interest rate? *South African Journal of Economics* 55.

Whittle, E.P., 1990. *Findings of a Survey of Problem Areas in South African Society.* Pretoria: HSRC.

Williamson, John, 1990. *The Progress of Policy Reform in Latin America.* Washington, D.C.: Institute for International Economics.

Wilson, F. and M. Ramphele, 1989. *Uprooting Poverty: The South African Challenge.* Cape Town: David Philip.

World Bank, 1988. *World Development Report 1988.* Oxford University Press: New York.

World Bank, 1990. *World Development Report 1990.* Oxford: Oxford University Press.

Wynia, Gary W., 1978. *Argentina in the Postwar Era.* Albequerque: University of New Mexico Press.

Zimbalist, Andrew, 1989. Incentives and planning in Cuba. *Latin American Research Review* 24.

Zimmermann, Horst, 1981. Internationale Finanz und Steuerbelastungsvergleiche. In: Alber, Willi (ed.). *Handwörterbuch der Wirtschaftswissenschaft (HdWW)*, vol. 3.

Index